for Shahalla
Shahlla

Living for the
Sake of the Soul

*with infinite love
and joy!*

yogacharya
O'Brian

Living for the Sake of the Soul

Ellen Grace O'Brian

CSE Press

Cover and book design: Clarice Hirata

Cover photograph of author: Ron Lindahn

First printing, 2016
ISBN Number: 978-0-692-77799-2
Library of Congress Catalog Number: 2016953419

Printed in the United States of America.

This book is printed on acid-free paper.

CSE Press
1146 University Avenue
San Jose, CA, 95126
1.408.283.0221
info@CSEcenter.org
www.CSEcenter.org

For all who embark upon the eternal way
of spiritually awakened living

CONTENTS

Foreword
Roy Eugene Davis

Among personal behaviors that can interfere with our innate urge to be fully, spiritually awake is the habit of being so involved with constantly changing mental and emotional conditions and outer circumstances that we are inclined to be Self- and God-forgetful.

Our true Self (soul) is a flawless, immortal unit of the pure essence of ultimate Reality. While we may be somewhat intuitively aware of what we are, we cannot be completely satisfied until we actually realize (directly experience and clearly know) it.

Until Self-realization is constant, it can be nurtured by discriminative Self-examination, prayer, constructive affirmation, regular meditation, rising above all small, egocentric perceptions of self-identity, and reading the inspired words of Self- and God-aware people.

Themes in this book can empower you to have your attention and awareness anchored in the Infinite as you wisely attend to duties and relationships and steadily grow to emotional and spiritual maturity.

Having known the author for more than thirty years and often presented meditation seminars at Center for Spiritual Enlightenment in San Jose, California, where she is the senior minister and spiritual director, I can attest to her complete dedication to encouraging others to learn to have ideal experiences and circumstances in all aspects of their lives.

Living for the *Sake of the Soul* can be helpful to all readers who sincerely endeavor to live effectively and fervently aspire to be spiritually enlightened.

—*Roy Eugene Davis*

Introduction

*Spiritual practices, those seemingly small acts
we commit to each day, are the threads that tie
our life into a meaningful whole.*
—from *A Single Blade of Grass*

Besides being a writer by nature, I am someone who
loves to read and to study. Fortunately for me, the
path of Kriya Yoga encourages that. It is one of the
core disciplines—to read, then meditate and contemplate spiritual teachings every day. I often take notes
and in a sense, talk to myself. I reflect out loud on
paper. I think of ways to take note of what matters,
what I want to remember, how I most want to live.

For more than a decade, these short statements
or reminders for living a spiritually-conscious life
have been shared with others as *Daily Inspirations*.
They are written on the chalkboard in the meditation
garden at CSE headquarters every day of the year
and read by visitors to the garden who stop to meditate and take in the beauty of the place, or by those
attending worship services, classes, or a meditation
retreat. Situated near the fountain in the courtyard in
front of the temple, the inspiration board is a natural
place to stop, to look, and then to listen to one's own
heart. The same messages are also sent daily via email
to thousands of subscribers who read them as a way

to begin the day with inspiration when they start up their computers.

Frequently, I receive notes of astonishment or appreciation from readers regarding the timeliness or poignancy of a particular message of the day. Sometimes email subscribers remark that they feel the message was uniquely designed just for them. I am deeply grateful for the many devotees of God, from many different faiths and spiritual paths, different countries and cultures, different stages and walks of life, who partake of *Daily Inspirations,* yet I have not written for them. These inspirational notes are my own practice reminders. And perhaps because they are personal and mined from the cave of my own sadhana, they may resonate with others on the path of awakening. That is my prayer.

These inspirations are drawn from the well of ancient Vedic wisdom and brought into the context of our 21st-century lives. The philosophy and practices of the Kriya Yoga tradition as passed on to me from my teacher, Roy Eugene Davis, are focused on the importance of spiritual awakening—how we each can realize the truth of what we are as spiritual beings and live our lives in harmony with that. One Ultimate Reality is the source and substance of all that is— which includes every one of us. Every person, every living being, everything that exists, is an expression of It. Because we are That, our essential Self is already spiritual, already whole and complete.

True to the spirit of the wise saying from the *Rig Veda—Truth is one; the sages call It by various names*—you will find many names for that one Reality in this volume. Whether referred to as Ultimate Reality, Supreme Consciousness, God, Spirit, Self, Source, or Truth, that Truth is one and the same.

The path of spiritual awakening is a process of Self-unfoldment, or revelation of essential truth. All of our disciplines—our daily meditation and prayer, study, and healthy lifestyle choices are simply to remove anything that would obscure our accurate perception and full expression of the true Self. Nothing needs to be attained or added on to us in order for us to be enlightened. Our efforts do not create a spiritual condition, they only reveal what is so. And, once we realize the truth, our discipline becomes natural. It becomes the way we live. It allows our inner peace and innate bliss, the joy of the soul, to permeate everything. Our priorities become clear and we live with higher purpose. This is living for the sake of the soul.

The four main parts of this book mirror key insights into Vedic philosophy: There is one Reality; we are all expressions of It; we tend to become identified with body and mind and forgetful of the unseen divine Self; and ultimately, we awaken to the truth of our being and realize our innate wholeness—that is our certain destiny. However, just as there is no real boundary between what we truly are and what we must discover, so there is no true division for the sayings. They are all about awakening—about realizing the essential Self and living a fulfilled, meaningful life. This means you can open the book anywhere and ideally, find something useful or inspiring.

The sayings found in *Living for the Sake of the Soul,* like the encouraging words of the *Daily Inspirations* they are drawn from, are meant to be spiritual practice reminders. Any one of them can stand alone, and taken together you will find a river of associated themes. There are many ways to explore a river! Look at the map, take a hike to the shore, get in a boat and set out, wade in, or jump in and swim. This book can be explored in similar ways. You might start with the table of contents to see which topic is the right one for you as a point of entry. Or peruse the volume, reading along until you find a stopping place, a saying that bids you to stay awhile. Or, one of my favorite ways to explore a book of inspirations, *just jump in.* Open it randomly and look at the page you landed on.

There are just as many ways to practice with this book as there are to read it. Setting the book near your meditation seat, to be available for a moment of reflection after meditating, when the thinking mind is calm, discernment is clear, and intuition is awakened, can facilitate contemplation. Or next to your bed, in that spot reserved for the last moments of uplifting and prayerful thought at day's end. Just as I wrote these sayings to help me remember and clarify my own understanding of the teachings, I hope you will do the same. Read them, then write. Clarify your own insights and goals. Above all, find your own way—that is the heart of the heart of the teachings.

This collection of sayings is possible due to the generosity, compassion, and dedication of many souls. My beloved guru, Roy Eugene Davis, remains a font of divine inspiration for me and countless others. I am profoundly grateful for the clarity of the teachings he has selflessly and freely offered for many decades and for his kind and wise foreword for this book. The selected sayings from the sages of Kriya Yoga that begin each part of the book were drawn from Mr. Davis' book, *Seven Lessons in Conscious Living,* published by CSA Press.

I am so appreciative of the many inspired companions along the way who have valued these sayings and helped others have access to them. Steve Dharma Hall, who many years ago suggested, and then made it possible, to send *Daily Inspirations* over the internet, setting them up to be the dawning inspiration for people to start their day; Parthenia Kavita Hicks, who brought her poetic heart and editing mind to allow these sayings to become a book; Dr. Genie Palmer, who gathered the sayings from the years of archives as if they were precious gems; Rev. Sundari Jensen, who through the years has continued to make sure the inspirations get posted on the chalkboard every day and Holly Gray, who posts them on our website to set sail around the globe; Rev. Bev Rajni Kam, who edited many sayings over the years; Ron Lindahn, who offered his creative photography skill for the author photo for the book cover; Clarice Hirata, the designer for the cover and inside pages of the book, whose sensitive listening and graphic design talent continue to amaze me, even after decades of working together; Rev. Shawne Anandamayi Smith, who used a magnifying glass to search out and find duplicate entries that were hiding in the manuscript; Kate Sheehan Roach, who brought her editing skill and light of inspiration in at the eleventh hour; Sue Evanicky, and all of the volunteers, whose selfless dedication makes CSE Press possible; and all those who stop in the garden to read, subscribe online, or read this collection, who take them to heart, share with a friend, or from time to time send me a note— thank you from my heart.

May you find in these pages some glimpses of divine possibility for your life, encouragement to remain steadfast on your path of spiritual awakening, and clear reminders of the magnificent truth of your being.

—Ellen Grace O'Brian

One Reality is the Life of All

Very few people know that the wholeness of God extends fully to this physical realm.

—Mahavatar Babaji

Seek the Truth

Put God first.

• • •

Each day at dawn and at dusk your divine Beloved opens the door of peace and invites you in. The whole earth meditates then.

• • •

Do everything as worship, make every act an offering. The conscious awareness of the omnipresence of God will fill your heart and mind day and night.

• • •

Practice meeting all people and all situations with the awareness that you are meeting your Self. Assume basic goodness and transform even the most difficult relationships. Let the truth of your being meet the truth of another. The key to right relationship with everyone is respect based on oneness—the conscious realization that there is only one Reality. Our relationships provide a precious opportunity for spiritual awakening. Behold the Divine in all people and in all situations.

• • •

With spiritual maturity we stop asking God to fix things for us. Instead, we learn to "lean into the light," to cultivate the conscious awareness of spiritual sufficiency and divine grace already at work in our life. We see through the chaos of challenges by affirming that a higher harmony is unfolding. We bring that inner harmony into expression—first through our faith in the transformative power of Spirit, then through our conscious cooperation to do the next right thing we know to do. Through it all, we trust that all is well. This keeps our mind clear and our heart receptive to the divine guidance that is waiting to pour forth and fill the chalice of our consciousness.

• • •

The ability to listen is more valuable than the ability to speak. Consider that God is speaking to you today. Listen carefully. Listen with your ears, your eyes, your feelings, your intuition, your body, your heart. There are so many ways to listen for the One that is everywhere at all times.

• • •

Striving to fix the world is arrogance. Instead, let us love the world as our Self and strive to change any part of our own life that does not reflect this truth.

• • •

Be immersed in the light of divine remembrance. When the mind rests in divine consciousness we are free from worry and despair. Be an alchemist and transform all thoughts into thoughts of God, the one Reality. The debris of mundane ruminations that dull the mind will instead shine forth as the golden joy of divine realization.

• • •

Intuition is the tool that unlocks the wisdom of the scriptures. Approach the study of scripture knowing that spiritual knowledge is already within you. Read a little, then reflect. Allow your intuition to reveal deeper meanings and personal guidance.

• • •

We are all working on our master's degrees. We are here to attain spiritual mastery—to consciously live in the freedom and joy of the soul, fulfill our destiny, and make a positive contribution to life. The curriculum is to study your self. Observe the connection between thoughts, beliefs, and experiences. With mature spirituality the need for outer approval gives way to the difficult task of searching diligently within—finding and claiming the inner authority of the true Self.

• • •

We do not have to concern ourselves with being holy or happy. We only have to look for the mental barriers we have constructed that cover our radiant Self. Release them—wholeness and happiness are naturally revealed. Discovering the sacred in our life requires fresh eyes—seeing things as they are and not as we think, want, or assume them to be. The ability to transform our lives and our relationships is contained in something as simple as the way we perceive.

• • •

Fault-finding can be a habit, but so can approaching life with gratitude. We need only intend to be grateful and then train ourselves to look for the good. Soon, we notice more to be thankful for.

• • •

Why look for outer conditions to change in order to declare yourself prosperous, to declare yourself happy and successful? Do not wait; accept your spiritual inheritance now. There is a perfect and complete idea of fulfillment for your life; it can be no other way, as God is the source and substance of all that is. Remember: God is your life.

• • •

Seek Truth. Never be afraid to know it.
It will always nourish you.

• • •

Spiritual study combines meditation, contemplation, and application. To gather information without reflection and without putting into practice what we learn is like eating too much without properly digesting the food. The body cannot use it and soon it poisons the system, even if what was taken in was nutritious to begin with. Read, contemplate, and engage in active research. Let your daily life be a laboratory of self-study.

• • •

Prayer is a still activity, the perfect balance between doing and not-doing. Effective prayer is not sending out our thoughts to connect with God; it is rather an emptying of self so that the grace-filled activity of God can flow into our consciousness. The goal of prayer is not to change any circumstance, but to raise our understanding to a spiritual perspective and change our consciousness. With a transformed consciousness, we live in a new way. That is what changes things.

• • •

When we pray, the mind begins to seek truth. Once we enter the chamber of communion with the higher Self, problems fall away. When we consciously abide in truth, beyond mental struggle, the sense of separate self dissolves and prayer is answered. To develop a prayer life, we have to value prayer by knowing its worth. When we do, we can answer the call to prayer that comes many times throughout the day. First we turn to prayer. Then prayer turns us.

• • •

Information hoarded by the mind without connecting with the heart is like a powerful engine without spark plugs. How can it take us anywhere? The spiritual knowledge we acquire becomes wisdom when it transforms our will for good.

• • •

Prayer can take the form of simply being present to feelings and listening for divine insight within the depths of our heart, mind, and body. Divine intelligence and power pervades our entire being. Every cell is alive with the radiance of Spirit. Whatever we are currently experiencing in the body/mind can be a doorway to the Infinite by noticing what has energy, what captivates our attention. Go there with respectful curiosity; let it open to what is beyond.

• • •

Grace abounds everywhere like the air we breathe or like the grass that persistently grows beneath the sidewalk until it breaks through a crack. To recognize grace, we slow down and learn to look, cultivate humility and gratitude. Let your mind be immersed in God throughout the day by silent prayer, noticing seeming coincidences and all manner of divine support. With a receptive heart, you will begin to perceive grace astoundingly, pervasively present. When we begin to recognize grace, we wonder why it took us so long to notice. How did it escape our radar? We were not yet attuned to the subtle frequency of God's omnipresence.

• • •

Practice inquiry into truth. So many thoughts arise but few are grounded in truth. Learn to see thoughts as ephemeral clouds passing in the sky. Joy will permeate your life.

• • •

Knowledge about God is not Absolute Reality. It can be a doorway to Ultimate Truth but only if we go through it and leave it behind. When Absolute Reality is revealed, even the knower disappears.

• • •

There is a response to every soul call, guidance for every seeker of truth, a solution to every problem, and an answer to every prayer. To receive that answer, find that solution, or hear that guidance, recognize the one divine Reality that is with you now. In the silence of our soul, the Lord of Love knows even those dreams we leave unspoken. That divine power will light the way to their manifestation.

• • •

The experiences that seemed real to us while dreaming are seen as passing phenomena in the light of awakening. Use that insight to examine experiences in your waking life. They also will pass. Notice what remains.

• • •

Genuine curiosity is a great friend to a seeker of truth. Be curious when you pray for insight or understanding to be revealed. Expect that it will. Revelation is the unfolding of innate soul knowledge. If we do not divorce our spiritual self-inquiry from our daily life and responsibilities, we discover every situation can be a book of life from which we may study and learn. The sweet willingness of a truly curious mind is an invitation for revelation.

• • •

The Soul-Guided Life

Are you wondering what to do? The universe is divinely ordered. It allows us to fulfill our dharma, the law of our own nature, with the very opportunities now at hand. To discern the divine pattern that wants to unfold, we must see with the eyes of the heart as well as with the mind, with intuition as well as logic. Too often we rely on only one without the benefit the other can bring. Ask your heart, use your mind, intend to cooperate with the Infinite.

• • •

The road to joy is paved with surrender.

• • •

Gratitude is an approach to life that frees us from unconscious reactions to likes and dislikes. It supports the experience of equanimity and the realization that life is good. There is always something to be grateful for. Why not focus there? Start the day with an affirmative thought. Live the day with confidence in the Infinite. Conclude the day with appreciation for blessings you experienced.

• • •

When we follow the inclination to be generous, there is always enough. Generosity never fails to nourish us and those around us. It flows from the truth of who we are like the cooling waters of a mountain spring.

• • •

Devotion to God softens the heart and brings sweetness to meditation. Rote technique without devotion is like a dry creek bed. The banks are there but the flow of water is missing. Cultivate devotion and the subtle flow of divine vital force will bring new life and energy to your meditation practice. Like grasses after the spring rain, a new freshness will arise.

• • •

The soul-guided life radically reorders our priorities and transforms our way of responding to circumstances. It invites us to love when logic would have us hate; to forgive when we would be inclined to resent; to risk when we want to draw back in fear; to make amends when pride would have us demand an apology; to give when we feel poor; to choose a higher security than money can bring. Soar through your day on the wings of faith. Keep turning your mind to God. Soon it will return to remembrance of God on its own, as a bird rides the current home.

• • •

What is it to be willing to let God lead? Think of it as being completely open to divine support. To welcome divine guidance, we cultivate the willingness to venture beyond the limits of what is comfortable and familiar and let ourselves be guided by truth.

• • •

To meditate, use the power of the mind itself to subdue restless thoughts. This is accomplished through intention, focus, and ultimately, surrender. Intend to commune with God, focus your attention on a single point, gently ignore thoughts that arise, and surrender the sense of separation by letting go into the allness of God's presence right where you are.

• • •

To see clearly, journey within to "the mountain of God." Discover your place of solitude, the higher consciousness where thoughts cannot intrude. When restless thoughts subside and you experience clear awareness, let your attention remain there. When you reach the summit of inner peace, stay awhile. Luxuriate in the expansiveness of Supreme Consciousness.

• • •

The bird that neglects to visit the flower misses the nectar. Daily practice of prayer and meditation opens our heart, purifies our mind, and introduces us to the sweetness of divine communion.

• • •

Have you imagined that meditation is stopping all thoughts? That is like trying to stop the wind. Let the wind be while you take shelter in the stillness of the Self. Thoughts may continue but they need not disturb you or interrupt your meditation. The wind doesn't blow all day. Eventually it quiets down. Give no regard to thought activity and it will subside.

• • •

Imagine, or feel, that sitting in meditation is sitting in the grace-bestowing presence of the One. Just sit. Feel that with each breath you are being blessed.

• • •

There are three types of prayers:
Where are you?
Please help.
Thank you.

• • •

Let your heart sing with the joy of surrendered devotion. Inwardly bow at the feet of the divine One you meet in every encounter. No earthly pleasures, or worldly treasures can compete with the swell of gratitude that arises from the awareness of the pervasive presence of that Reality which is the life of all.

• • •

To be effective, prayer must move from talking to God to listening to God—being receptive to divine inspiration. Be willing to pause for a prayer moment any time the inclination arises. Watch for it. Look for the prayer windows that open and gaze through them into awareness of the infinite presence of God.

• • •

Practice radical humility by being open to greatness. We are each here according to divine purpose and that is magnificent, indeed. If we are open to it, we continually feel its pull to live in a higher way. An ache in the heart or a prompting from the soul calls to us to awaken to the truth of what we are. Have courage. Be receptive to what that is and then live it.

• • •

We search for truth in prayer by placing our attention on that which is real in the absolute sense and letting that which is changeable fade away. If it is health that you seek, or love, or prosperity, let it go as a condition you are searching for. Instead, put your attention on the infinite fullness of divine Reality within you. Let the spiritual experience of wholeness provide a change in consciousness. The most effective prayer we can experience is to pray all the way through the condition until our sense of human lack, limitation, and problems drop away and we simply rest in the divine truth of our own wholeness. When our consciousness is illumined by the spiritual truth of our being, healing is revealed.

• • •

Opening up to our vulnerabilities can lead us toward awakening. We all have a unique link to our divine connection. This link is not our perfection, but our imperfection; not what we can do but what we cannot do; not where we are well-adjusted, but where we are broken open; not where we are proud but where we are humble. For the devotee of God, vulnerabilities are the places where divine grace slips in and accomplishes for us what we cannot do for ourselves. Then we know.

• • •

To decide on a course of action, first take time to become established in the awareness of the presence of God. Let divine peace fill your mind. Then inwardly inquire, *What is in harmony with the highest good?*

• • •

Spend time in nature today. Let its vitality and beauty nourish your body and mind. Do not try to accomplish anything during this time. Just walk and wander, or sit and rest. Notice what captivates your attention. Recognize the one Reality in all you observe. Be consciously immersed in That.

• • •

When we attempt to practice spiritual surrender—letting go of the illusion that we are separate from the one Reality—it may take a while to let go of our habitual clinging to ego identity. Yet we will discover that we cannot stop God's incessant grace from breaking down the barriers to truth. How wonderful! Let go of any negative thoughts or beliefs about your ability to surrender—those belong to ego anyway. Such thoughts are about the past. Today is the day to begin again. The past is gone; this is your day to be fully awake.

• • •

The great secret of bhakti yoga, the practice of devotion to God, is knowing that there is only one relationship in life. All relationships are expressions of that. How can we accomplish single-minded devotion to God in the midst of work and family life? See God in all. Serve God in all.

• • •

Faith is a whole-hearted "yes." It says, *I may not know how this can be accomplished, but I am willing to trust Spirit to guide me each step of the way, one step at a time.* We attain what our heart is fixed upon.

• • •

Selfless service may look the same on the outside as service that comes from a place of self-serving, but inside the heart is different. With selfless service, there is no grasping, pushing, or desiring. Engaging in selfless service can free us from worry and anxiety and open us to pure joy. It is the only way to realize freedom in action.

• • •

Every day serve with love; give God your all. Every night completely release all you have done and experienced; turn it over to God. Each day is new; begin anew. Do not worry; God is your ever-present support.

• • •

Finding fault is easy. Often it is just an old habit that drags us down. All day long the lower brain looks for threats like an early cave dweller scanning the horizon for predators. To interrupt this insistent tendency, we can train our brain to look for the good, to seek out what is uplifting and can be affirmed. Decide to notice and inwardly affirm what you find praiseworthy. Before falling asleep at night, take a few moments to engage your memory in a positive scan of the day. What went right? What useful or healthy choices did you make? Even if you can only think of one positive thing, focus on that and magnify it. Reflect on how it felt and what that positive experience was like. Our health, our sense of well-being, and our relationships all benefit from this change of focus. So simple, so powerful.

• • •

Guidance for healthy living shines continuously from the wisdom of the soul, yet sense attachments and their friends, self-will and habit, may overshadow it. Pause for a moment to seek the soul's wisdom before taking action. Develop the habit of "the conscious pause," a moment of checking in with your higher Self before speaking or acting. Life is more pleasant this way.

• • •

Discernment often requires the willingness to actively wait with faith for clarity. Faith is our ability to wait with positive expectation of revelation. Faith holds the time of not knowing as a fisherman holds his line.

• • •

Pray fearlessly. Put aside self-doubt and claim your most precious relationship—that of the soul with Spirit. Why be a beggar when the kingdom is yours? Claim, demand, assert your divine inheritance—the jewels of Self-realization.

• • •

For a relationship to thrive we must give our time and attention to it. We must make ourselves available for intimacy, those moments when the light of love is revealed. Our relationship with God is no different. Meditation is one way to cultivate intimacy with God. With meditation we make ourselves available to realize God, not only as our divine companion, but as our life. The most intimate experience possible— oneness with the One.

• • •

Dwell in Possibility

What turns the mind toward the light of awakening but the presence of divine light Itself?

• • •

We cannot know God with the mind. We can think about God but thoughts are inherently limited, unable to contain the unbounded Infinite. Yet the sages tell us that God can be known. How? Through direct experience. In superconscious meditation, when thoughts become still and awareness rests in our essence of being, God can be realized.

• • •

Everything gives according to its nature; nothing can provide more than what it is. What is temporary brings temporary happiness or security, which is its full extent. Only That which is eternal can give lasting happiness. O Seeker! Make friends with That.

• • •

God's grace sustains us; the guru's grace opens us to possibility; our own grace frees us.

• • •

We are all potential conduits for the awakening of planetary consciousness. When it is time for a divine idea to be expressed, Spirit finds a willing vehicle. We can choose to cooperate with divine will or not. Regardless of what we choose, it will find a way. Consciously participating in global awakening is signing up for our own transformation.

• • •

There is enough for all in God's economy. Invest your awareness in knowledge of that. The dividends are infinite.

• • •

Everything in this world is a fast-moving current of change; only God remains changeless. Rely on God alone for support in every situation. Sometimes people wonder how to do that. Start by knowing, or even imagining, you have an invisible means of support. Include other people who assist as well as helpful circumstances that come forth in your awareness of support, even as you inwardly remember the one source of it all.

• • •

Om, the primordial sound, the emanation of divine creative power, pervades the world. Everyone and everything resounds with Om. Meditate on Om, the life-giving and transforming inner sound. It is the source of all sound, the ultimate mantra. Contemplate it—be consciously immersed in it and yearn to know what is beyond it. What is the source of divine creative power and energy?

• • •

A single-minded focus on truth—the intention to live in harmony with the higher true Self—quickly and profoundly simplifies our spiritual path. With that steadfast commitment, no special seminars, books, or organizing techniques are needed for us to observe a more spiritually uplifting life. What we need is already within us.

• • •

Imagine the freedom of living in the soul—able to perceive and spontaneously respond to the promptings of inner guidance. No confusion or doubt, just clarity. An awakened heart, an illumined mind, free from attachment or aversion, open to the graces of the present moment. Imagine.

• • •

All right work serves God. Think of God in all that you do, whether you feel content or unhappy in your present work. Never lose sight of God and God will direct your path to new horizons of service.

• • •

Fill your life with thoughts of God by considering that everything is coming to you from God. Remember that you are doing everything for, and in, that divine Reality. When you relate to other people, relate to them spiritually. In this way, our lives are filled with the awareness of God as ever-present, like the air we breathe.

• • •

Prayer is necessary food for a healthy heart and mind. It aligns body, mind, and spirit. With it, we can keep our balance. Without it, one part of our nature is compromised and another over-developed. With prayer naturally comes humility, then everything else falls into place.

• • •

The moment we begin making a spiritual effort, grace comes to support our endeavors and propel us forward on the path.

• • •

With prayer we enter the open moment, the realm of all possibility. It gives us the ability to see in the darkness with the light of faith.

• • •

Contemplate wholeness. When you meditate, intend to experience it, to allow all barriers to fall away. No blessing, no grace, no power, or healing energy is ever withheld or missing from our life.

• • •

Be ever attentive to the "divine ache" in the soul that longs for God throughout your day. Then you will be ready when awareness of the divine One comes to you through a kind word, the beauty of nature, a moment of insight, or a synchronous event.

• • •

The eternally-creative, life-giving power of God expresses as every soul. This power is within us. It does not take us to prosperity. It is prosperity. To prosper is to realize and express our innate wholeness.

• • •

Every thought is a prayer. Every word is a blessing. Every action is a meditation. When daily meditation and conscious activity work together in our lives, the line that separates them disappears. Our life becomes our meditation.

• • •

Our certain destiny is freedom—the liberation of our consciousness from ignorance of our true nature. When we walk toward freedom, divine grace supports us, but we have to take that step. Readiness for that step is at hand when we discern that despite our persistent efforts to find lasting happiness, it continues to elude us. We begin to sense that what we are looking for is different, something that cannot be found in the ordinary way. We may not yet know how it is to be found, but we are willing to follow our yearning and step toward it.

• • •

Regardless of any harmful deeds we may have done, the true Self remains unstained.

• • •

Those who are devoted in their efforts to find God ultimately discover that they have been carried by God's grace all along. That infinite Reality we call God has always pervaded our life; it could never be lost or missing. All that we have, all that we are, all that we need, comes to us in and through Divine Consciousness.

• • •

Any and every time we engage in spiritual practice, it is a manifestation of God's grace. Consider this: what calls us to prayer, meditation, or moments of gratitude? Only God.

• • •

Life and death are not the pairs of opposites we might imagine them to be. Birth and death are the opposites—coming and going. Life is the eternal continuum that contains them both.

• • •

Drink the ecstatic wine of divine communion
from the cup of the present moment.

• • •

To experience the real solution to a problem, enter the temple of spiritual truth beyond words and thoughts. Sit in the silence, receptive to your soul's inspiration. It will come.

• • •

We are in the midst of the divine play. The divine Friend continually invites us to see a larger view of this life we are living. Clues and prompts are everywhere. When we pay attention, we discover it. Life is holy; heaven is here.

• • •

Grief is a doorway to divine love. When grief is encountered, embraced, and released consciously, it leads to the experience of the all-pervading presence of the One. Nothing can come between us and divine love and support. It is always present.

• • •

Contemplate the eternal Reality beyond changing appearances. Why settle for a spectator's seat in the theater of life? Go backstage and become intimate friends with the Producer.

• • •

One conscious breath can change your mind.

• • •

For some, devotion means love for God. For others, devotion is dedication to truth. In either case, the commitment of devotion attracts revelation. Our yearning proceeds from a glimmer of our innate knowing that leads back to its source.

• • •

Our consciousness, our body, mind, and soul—the totality of our being—is the dwelling place of God. The divine guidance we seek is there. What do you want to know? Begin with the bold and true assertion that as an expression of God, all knowledge is within you. Be receptive, be curious and expect guidance to be revealed. It will.

• • •

The gap between what we are called to be, or to do, and what we believe we are capable of, is where the grace of God enters. Consider that we would not even have a higher calling unless God was already at work in our life.

• • •

We live in an abundant universe, full of creative power, energy, and grace. Abundance is not something that we create for ourselves or have at the expense of others. Recognize that abundance is at hand and within the natural order of life. Life is capable of bringing forth whatever is needed to fulfill its purposes. When we let go of clinging to any idea of lack and instead turn our gaze toward the limitless sufficiency of Spirit, we can see this.

• • •

Seek out the soul's medicine for whatever ails you. The quickening of soul awareness brings us back to life; it raises us up and heals what is dead in us—in our personal lives, our institutions, and our communal life. Spiritual realization revives what has burned out and restores hope where it was lost.

• • •

True beauty does not seek to conform to outer standards. Because it is not concerned with itself, it is a transparent opening for the light of divine beauty to shine through.

• • •

Surrender is accepting that God is all.

• • •

All things move and change in time, then find rest and renewal in the eternal stillness of Spirit. When we are anchored in that stillness, we can notice what is ready to move out of our life and let it go gracefully.

• • •

Inwardly walk through the chapel door of God's omnipresence and experience yourself praying "in" God rather than "to" God. Know that God is nearer than your heartbeat, the essence of your being. See with the eye of spiritual wisdom, the One that is you, the One life of all.

• • •

The Flowering of Self-Knowledge

Bliss arises from the soul. This unconditional joy is not emotion. It is the flowering of Self-knowledge that frees us from fear, envy, grief, or greed. The darkness of ignorance flees in the light of Self-knowledge.

• • •

Seeing the one life in all is recognizing the body of God. As our own body has different parts but belongs to one organism, so with spiritual vision we see everyone and everything as one interconnected life. The tiniest insect, the majestic mountains, our beloved family members, the billions of souls living on this earth we have never met and even those beyond—all the body of God. The holy temple is everywhere.

• • •

Generosity always returns generosity. What we send forth is what comes back to us. Do not be fooled when it comes back another way, seemingly unrelated to the gift you gave. Life is one seamless whole, ever responsive to our thoughts and actions.

• • •

See through the veil of differences to the unity of life. People have different talents and abilities but at the soul level, there is absolute equality. Everyone deserves the same respect; all are expressions of the one Reality. Look through all appearances and relate to others soul to soul. As this conscious relationship is courted, the field of God reveals itself to the devotee as omnipresent and infused with supportive grace. This brings such joy to the heart that praise for all that is naturally arises within us.

• • •

Faith develops over our lifetime as we persevere with vigorous intent on the spiritual path and are met time and again by the presence of grace. The first discipline of faith is to notice divine support. Be aware of the ways you feel connected to the larger Reality, such as the occurrence of synchronicities, insights, revelations, or unexpected but timely support. When you see it, do not ignore it or brush it off. Lift it up. Magnify it—let it bring peace to your mind and joy to your heart.

• • •

God's will speaks silently in the receptive soul,
  gracefully leading toward inspired action.

• • •

Contemplation of Om, the primordial sound vibration emanating from the expressive aspect of ultimate Reality, purifies the mental field. Absorbing our attention in this inner sound during meditation brings mastery of the senses, mental clarity, and prepares us for direct insight into our essential nature.

• • •

Real peace in our lives cannot be created; it has no cause. It is an unconditional spiritual quality that is innate to the soul. Revealed when our lives are in balance and we act with integrity, it makes the blossoming of the inspired life possible. Seek peace first in the garden of your soul. Be like the songbird perched on the top of the tree whose song fills the garden and inspires those passing by.

• • •

Spiritual knowledge amassed only from books is like a house built of cards—a little troublesome wind will overturn it. But knowledge gained through direct perception is unshakable. Seek God in the book of your heart through daily, divine meditation.

• • •

Discipleship is reorienting our life toward Self- and God-realization. It is learning to be Self-reliant, rather than looking outside ourselves for support, freedom, joy, or security. Instead of a purely external point of reference, discipleship acquaints us with the fountain of infinite life within us. We come to know our own wholeness as the unfailing source of our security and abiding happiness. When the divine Self is our moment-to-moment experience, we are not swayed by differing spiritual systems of thought or practice. One who relies on externals will always be chasing after the next spiritual experience or the newest teacher on the scene. Such seekers remain unfulfilled until they awaken to the divine Reality within.

• • •

There are many things in life we can accomplish with simple will power or effort, but the unfolding of our highest potential requires our cooperation with grace. Intend to cooperate with divine will and grace will meet you at every turn. Grace knows no effort or cost, no merit or reason. It is the gift of divine support given freely. We cannot earn grace but we can open ourselves to it, like the flower that turns toward the sun.

• • •

Divine guidance rarely specifies what we should do. Instead, it comes as peace. It comes as love. It comes as truth. It comes bearing our divine nature itself. "Here," it says. "Abide here." And if we will but abide there, in that experience of wholeness, specific guidance comes exactly when it is needed. Divine timing is rarely ego's timing. There is a palpable distinction, like the difference between pushing on a closed door trying to open it and one that opens as you approach it.

• • •

When you pray, let divine peace fill your heart, mind, and body. Trust that your every prayer is answered, every need filled. Let your imagination soar. Accept that you are infinitely creative as you open yourself to divine possibility. The abundant blessings of divine supply appear as we depend on them, as we move toward our dreams with confidence in the infinite resourcefulness of Spirit. Every good thing that is intended for us according to God's grace comes to us; nothing can prevent it.

• • •

Spiritual truth lifts each one of us out of the constraints of perceived separation and limitation. It appears through divine grace in a way unique to every person, opening us to the direct experience of spiritual power and presence. We know grace when we experience it because we feel awe, or a kind of tearful joy, a fullness that renders us momentarily speechless. We feel blessed, healed, expanded, and lifted up. The experience of divine grace is a glimpse behind the veil of separation, a vision of wholeness that frees us from fear. Grace is a taste of God that we never forget.

• • •

The vision of oneness naturally leads to compassionate action and service of humanity because we see the pain and joy of others as our own. Just as we are instinctively inclined to care for our own body when it is injured, so one who is awake cannot resist caring for others. Everyone walks on the spiritual path; there is no other. This path is reciprocity. When we discover that, the journey of awakening begins.

• • •

The fire of divine love that burns in the devotee's heart can be used in three ways: as a light of worship, bringing awareness to God's omnipresence; as the warmth of generosity, serving God in all; and as the fire of self-discipline, using self-restraint to purify our thoughts, words, and actions for the soul's bright expression.

• • •

We become the meeting place of heaven and earth as we open to divine ideas and bring them into manifestation. Look to the Source first to supply your needs. Ask in secret, in consciousness, then let your awareness expand beyond any need into the boundless nature of the Self. Insights and inspiration will flow from the fount of divine communion and you will attract what is needed to realize your dreams.

• • •

There is nothing essential missing in your life. There is no need to wander from room to room. Nothing needs to change for blessing to occur. Just learn how to look.

• • •

Supreme Consciousness
is Our True Nature

One Ultimate Reality is the source of everything. Souls are immortal; the attributes of Ultimate Reality are within them. Let your spiritual path be God-communion.

—Lahiri Mahasaya

Every Moment Wisdom

Are you looking for God?
God is your life.

• • •

Self-realization may at first seem to be a foreign and lofty term, as if we will discover some Self that we never knew. That which we are, have always been, and ever will be, is revealed. That is it. Those who are Self-realized know the essence of their own being as spiritual in nature. They see all of life as one Reality. Wherever they are, they are home—at one with the One.

• • •

We do not acquire spiritual realization; it is revealed from within. When we want to see in the dark we turn on a light. To see more clearly in life, we turn within and invite the illumination of our consciousness by intentionally abiding in the divine Self.

• • •

Have faith in your Self. Be happy. Serve others.

• • •

The true Self always has a way through difficulty even when the conditioned self cannot see a possibility for healing or reconciliation. Be open to that. Wait for its inspiration to break through in your troubled mind like the sunlight through the clouds.

• • •

The power of Spirit supports the production of the world and the changes in nature but remains ever unchanged by any of it. So it is with our own life and soul nature. While life is full of growth, decay, and change, the soul remains unmoved. Nothing can mar the soul or change it—not gain or loss, righteousness, or error. We are all eternally blessed with infinite life, knowledge, and joy. Expand your mind by thinking "eternally blessed."

• • •

Think of the soul first. Consider your life purpose in terms of who you really are rather than what you think you want to do. Concentrate on expressing your soul qualities. What is truly yours to do will be gracefully revealed.

• • •

Self- and God-realization, to know who we are and to realize God as the true Self of all, is the mystical bridge that connects the deepest wisdom of the world's religions. This is the "yugadharma," the law or duty, necessary for our time. To recognize our inter-dependent life through our common humanity and our shared divinity is the foundation for a healthy planet and a peaceful world.

• • •

Stories of the awakened ones such as Jesus or Buddha tell us that they sometimes remained silent when asked about Truth. Not because they did not know, but because they did. Ultimate spiritual realization is experienced beyond mind, beyond words and thoughts, in the silence of the soul. Speech cannot capture it; at best it can point to it.

• • •

The desire for Self-realization only arises through the power of God's grace. If you have the desire for spiritual awakening, then you already have grace-filled support—count on it, and move confidently in the direction of your dreams.

• • •

Being surrendered to God requires living in the moment, open to what life brings. This does not mean that we float along in our boat, tossed here and there with every wave of change, without steering toward a destination. Our course is charted to God-realization; our rudder is selfless service.

• • •

We find our greatest happiness in the open field of possibility, yet search endlessly for the shelter of certainty. Imagine living freely without restriction, forever conscious of your essential unbounded spiritual nature, abundantly contributing to the well-being of all. Feel this to be true now. Cultivate this joyful experience as your consciousness expands and your life more fully expresses your divine Self. Think of the bird that flies. First, the grip on the branch is released.

• • •

Cultivate good habits and good friends will follow.

• • •

If you want to please God, live this day with the intent to please your higher true Self. With each choice inquire, *Does this please the soul?* You will know.

• • •

Life is an ever-expansive present moment that we divide into past and future. Everything meets in this moment—the thoughts and deeds of our past, our present experience, and our future. The tree and its fruit live in the seed. Each day we plant the seeds of our future happiness. Be a wise spiritual farmer. Till the ground of mind and consciousness with faith and choose well the seeds you will nurture—the thoughts you will cultivate, the habits you will sow.

• • •

A storehouse of spiritual principles that can help us meet every real need is available to us. When we unlock this treasure through right understanding and put it into practice, peace and prosperity arrive to grace our days. Goal setting from the spiritual perspective starts with awareness of our inner resources. We recall that we are spiritual beings. We affirm the fullness that is inherently ours, rather than focus on what is missing. This perspective declares, *I am whole and complete.* We affirm what is possible and call it forth. The moment we earnestly intend something, it draws upon our inner resources and begins to express. We begin to attract to us what is needed and opportunities come to meet us at every turn.

• • •

Notice the abundant aliveness and divine intelligence continually pouring itself forth in nature. Even grasses once brown and dormant rise up with green vibrancy after the spring rain. This same healing power is inherent to our life and being.

• • •

We are Supreme Consciousness Itself. We look for well-being, but we are well-being. We search for wholeness, but we are wholeness. We desire prosperity and security. We already are that. We pray for love. We are love itself. Each moment, the door to spiritual fulfillment opens to us. We need only enter.

• • •

Goodness is innate to the soul. Forget trying to be good, that's like trying to be alive. Instead, put your focus on being authentic. Be true to your divine Self. How? Be lovingly aware of your divine nature. Let it express in all that you do. Do your own work and be attentive to your soul's joy. Let joy, the soul's delight, be your compass. If you lose touch with your bliss, it is time to recalibrate. Time to rechart your course.

• • •

We are each matchless expressions of Spirit, dwelling in the family of all beings. Our discipline in life is to cooperate with the Infinite and let it express uniquely through us. That is how we take our rightful place. We may look to others with admiration, or even jealousy, as we try to determine our niche in this world. But our place, our particular way of shining the light of Spirit, is specific to our individual life. Our body-mind constitution, life experiences, duties, talents, and the inclinations of our soul all contribute to the integral expression of Supreme Consciousness that we, alone, are. No one else can be that; no one else has the same life pattern. Being exactly who we are with appreciation for such an astounding opportunity is phenomenal. Remember you are a unique divine being; you cannot be compared to anyone else. We may emulate the good qualities and examples of others, but why imitate them? Free yourself to follow your path of realization by letting go of the idea that you should be like someone else. Who would want to miss the opportunity of a lifetime?

• • •

Live as a Spiritual Being

Spiritual practice cannot make us more spiritual. It cannot improve our essential Self. At the core of our being, we are already divine. We are perfect, whole, and complete. Our practice merely clears away any obstructions to perceiving the truth of what we are. Once we realize that, what was once spiritual practice becomes spiritually-conscious living.

• • •

Those seemingly small acts we commit to each day are the threads that tie our life into a meaningful whole. There is no use having a beautiful shell of an outer life if we have not cared for what really matters.

• • •

Bodies are temporary and continually undergoing change. This is easy enough to observe. Yet the invisible soul ever remains unchanging. The body is just the dwelling place, like the house we live in. Ultimately, we will move out of that house. We can respect it, care for it, enjoy it, even love it, all the while realizing we are not the house we live in. It does not define or confine us. The radiant light of the essential Self shines through it all.

• • •

Live boldly in the world as a spiritual being. Rely on the infinite resourcefulness of Divine Consciousness. The activity of truth in your own mind and consciousness will inspire, guide, and provide for you. The teaching that what we need is within us, obviously does not refer to material goods; none of us has a house, car, or money inside us. Yet what we have is unlimited access to divine inspiration and creative potential, that if rightly used, will connect us to whatever we need.

• • •

Marvel at the life force within a seed of grass that breaks through the crack in the asphalt and grows. Such a tiny thing. Such a mighty force. Marvel at the divine life force within you, greater than any obstacle you may encounter.

• • •

Throughout time people have achieved mastery in all walks of life and risen above obstacles to greatness. What is the common factor? A single-minded devotion to the goal. The way of God-realization is the same—single minded focus on the goal of awakening. The same potential exists in all; the same grace is present, and the same necessity for dedication. Press on.

• • •

Whatever sorrow there is, whatever sickness there is, whatever hatred there is, whatever unrest there is, Spirit is stronger. The power of Truth rises up to meet every challenge. It is human nature to accept certain parts of our life and to reject others, to want only happiness and reject sorrow. But this may cause us to miss the blessings that hide behind distressing disguises. We need not fear them. Nothing can ever diminish the blessed nature of our being. Nothing.

• • •

The spiritual journey of Self-realization is the journey of a lifetime—the opportunity to discover creativity, wisdom, and compassion beyond what we have even considered possible. There is a reason why we dream—we are made of possibility. Our true Self is Supreme Consciousness—unbounded, pure birthless, deathless, eternal being.

• • •

Being at ease in our own life is a simple joy
of awakening.

• • •

That devotee whose mind is anchored in God even when others are anxious is like a white winter flower spreading the light of beauty on a grey stormy day.

• • •

To welcome divine guidance, we must cultivate the willingness to venture beyond the limits of what is comfortable and familiar and let ourselves be guided by truth. How do we know when guidance is correct? The soul's peace tells us. We feel it when the waves of worry and doubt subside. Even if the guidance leads us toward a difficult choice, if it is truly right for us, we experience that peace.

• • •

For a devotee of God, true surrender is revealed as joy in doing the work at hand. Whatever the work is, it becomes worship. It makes no difference if the worship offering is sweeping the floor, working at the computer, or performing a surgery to help someone heal. When we are conscious of devotion for God as we work, any task is our way of placing flowers on the altar. The flowers we offer are sweet thoughts of divine remembrance and the altar is our awakened heart, steeped in Self-knowing.

• • •

Strive physically, mentally, and spiritually to give all that you can, in the best way you can, and release any tendency to hold on to the results of your work. We do not have the power to control outcomes. There will always be a factor that is beyond our grasp or control. How do we deal with that? We work with integrity and offer the results to God. The easiest way to facilitate this offering is to intend that all of our actions are constructive, that they are uplifting for all and make a positive contribution to life.

• • •

We are not here to make a living but to be radiantly alive. We are here to fulfill our divine destiny—to wake up spiritually and serve life with our talents. The distracted mind will always say, *later*. But the soul insists, *now*. This is the time to focus on living the spiritual life.

• • •

Truthfulness is the highway to manifestation. When we live and speak the truth there is no conflict between Spirit, soul, mind, and matter. Without conflict, the inherent creative abilities of the soul manifest freely. What we think, dream, imagine, and believe, we can bring forth.

• • •

With Self-knowledge we can engage in work without being bound by it. Our identity is not caught up in what we do because we have a clear understanding of who we are. Our happiness or security does not depend on anything external.

• • •

Truth has always been, and will always be, the great teacher. There is no new spiritual truth, only the perennial wisdom arising again and again through the ages restated in the language of the times so that it may be heard. Yoga, or conscious union with Truth, brings complete stability—the ability to remain undisturbed by the currents of change or desire. Unshakable happiness is the result.

• • •

The still, small voice of revealed knowledge is perceived through the faculty of intuition. To receive inner guidance, sit attentively until the thought waves in the mind settle and the light of soul inspiration shines forth.

• • •

Good works can bring us to the door of God-realization, but only surrender and grace take us through.

• • •

Faith is awakened remembrance of the divine within the heart of the devotee. It causes the mind to search for God in all things as a mother remembers her child in her heart and instinctively searches for him in a crowd. The face of that child alone comes shining through to her. See the face of God wherever you go.

• • •

Devotees in search of truth follow different paths to God-realization. When something precious is lost, people respond according to their nature. Some will mourn and seek solace, some will begin to look where they think it might be found, others will inquire as to where it was last seen, and some will remain serene knowing it is all in divine order.

• • •

Any condition is subject to change whether it is our financial condition, our health, our relationships, or vocation. What underlies these situations—the substance, or the essence, at the root of them—is not changeable. It does not wax and wane. It is always full. Remembering this is the sure antidote to worry.

• • •

Happiness and sorrow are both reflections of internal states of consciousness. Nothing outside of us can be their cause. If things, people, or situations could cause happiness or sorrow, then everyone would perceive it the same way, but what brings happiness to one person may bring sorrow to another. Even though we have different experiences of it or approaches to it, we are all looking for the same happiness. We seek happiness that will not fail or disappoint us. Why would we try so hard to find that unconditional happiness? Because deep down, we know it exists. It just takes us a while to figure out where and how to find it. That lasting happiness is only available within us. Realize your essential Self—then joy will be your constant companion and your greatest happiness will be found. How strange that we look everywhere for this happiness when all the while we are carrying it with us.

• • •

Until the heart is satisfied, we want more and more. What satisfies the heart? Realization of the divine Self. Only That.

• • •

Cooperate with the Infinite

Connect with your soul and intend to act from it. When you do, you will feel a river moving in you, a boundless joy.

• • •

There is work for us according to our temperament, duty, destiny, and nature but what matters most is our realization of the essential Self. Our real job is discovering how to live truthfully—allowing the radiant divine Self to fully express.

• • •

Whenever we are ready to prosper, we can take up the discipline of delighting in truth. First, we discipline our mind to engage in introspection for greater understanding of truth, then discipline our speech and actions to bring forth new behavior in alignment with that insight. We choose actions that are consistent with our vision of a prosperous life. Capture the vision of your extraordinary life, then live it—thought by thought, word by word, action by action.

• • •

Take a vacation from the hard work of resisting your good. Instead of imagining yourself "getting away from it all," imagine experiencing the freedom and joy of living your life here and now as God supports, directs, and inspires you moment to moment. Relax into being.

• • •

We have the ability to ride the waves of change with grace and delight. We do this by learning how to expand our awareness to hold the opposites. Free from clinging to this or that, we awaken to equanimity.

• • •

Risk being hopeful. Hope is essential on the spiritual journey. We hope to know eternal life and experience unconditional joy only because we innately know it is possible for us. Take your hopes seriously.

• • •

Meditation is a radical form of Self-acceptance; it arranges our meeting with the true Self—the most important meeting we can have. Do not miss it.

• • •

Why hold back? Set yourself free to engage fully in life—work without unnecessary anxiety; love without trying to own or control; play without holding back; set goals and aim high; miss the mark and learn from your mistakes; experience pleasure and all the good that life can offer. Free yourself from unnecessary stress based on misunderstanding the true nature of things. Does the ocean hold back from the wave? Does the sun hold back its light?

• • •

We attract relationships and circumstances that are consistent with our consciousness—our deeply held beliefs, habitual thoughts, mental states, and level of spiritual realization. Aim high.

• • •

Refuse to be fooled by limiting conditions. When a potter forms clay into a vessel, what was once open space is then seen as space inside and space outside. Yet the space itself remains unchanged. Break the vessel and the limiting factors disappear. Our true nature as a spiritual being is limitless. Remember that.

• • •

How to get beyond the thickets of thought? One mindful breath at a time, enter the sanctuary of meditation. Move into that higher consciousness where conditioned thoughts, habits, and negative behaviors cannot enter. In the true Self, habits have no power and fears have no ground.

• • •

The misguided ego attempts to rule our life by fear and competition with others; the awakened soul rules by divine love and sees the One in all. Competition is not lost; it becomes play.

• • •

Get to know your innate joy by experiencing it regularly after meditation. Become good friends with it. Sit with joy every day, encourage it to hang around. Avoid thinking you cannot experience joy because of some situation or challenge. With a calm mind, affirm your blissful nature and let go of any beliefs that interfere with your ability to access it. Your innate joy will blossom with each conscious breath.

• • •

We are capable of doing many things at once, such as driving our car while having a conversation with our friend who is a passenger. We can listen to our friend and respond, all the while keeping our attention on the road with awareness of our destination. In this same way, it is possible to work in the world and fulfill our responsibilities while inwardly engaging in prayer.

• • •

Four things to enhance and build your energy: meditate every day; cultivate positive thoughts; focus your attention on what truly matters; live simply.

• • •

The soul nature is intended to reign as the sovereign director of body and mind. When we allow the senses to rule body and mind, the light of the soul is hidden away under the dross of desire. Under the soul's guidance, body and mind shine with the light of truth. Divine wisdom, perceived through our clarified intellect and faculty of intuition, continually illumines the path of wholesome choices, making it easy to live well.

• • •

When some part of our body is injured and we feel pain, we instinctively move to protect and heal it. As we awaken to our oneness with all of creation, this natural response grows beyond the boundary of self. It becomes compassionate action.

• • •

The atmosphere of effective prayer is infused with receptivity. How can we receive the answer to our prayer when we cling to what we think that answer should be? Release longing for desired outcomes. Instead, trust that the highest good is now and always unfolding in divine order. Open your mind and consciousness with absolute willingness to know a new thing, be guided in a different direction, or be inspired to stay the course.

• • •

The prayer to be God's instrument is not a passive prayer. It requires our willingness to speak the word, sing the song, mend the relationship, and do the work that is inspired.

• • •

Be the source of the blessing you seek. There are those who see the pain of life and not the blessings, those who look for blessings and find them here and there, and those who offer blessings to all and find them everywhere. We are here to express as life-giving spiritual beings, leaving trails of blessings wherever we go.

• • •

Perseverance on the path of Self- and God-realization is essential. In all things, remain ever conscious of the goal. Lose the word "can't" and all that is associated with it. Free yourself from small thinking by opening to the expanded consciousness of divine possibility. Keep the goal of Self-realization ever in the background of your mind. Let it provide a litmus test for all you seek to do. Will your choice support your goal of spiritual awakening?

• • •

Those who drink daily from the soul's well of bliss are not driven to seek gratification elsewhere. They are free.

• • •

Forgiveness is possible because of the inherent purity of the Self. Whatever has occurred, the divine Self remains unstained and unchanged. The body and the mind may become wounded, ache and suffer, yet the power for healing continually arises from our essential Self. Remembering our pristine whole-ness, knowing there is that inviolable essence which can never be harmed, opens us to the possibility of forgiveness. When we offer forgiveness to others, we give ourselves the gift of freedom.

• • •

When young people taste the truth of the divine presence, when they feel compassion, when they know the joy that comes through serving, and when they feel the passion of what it is like to live a spiritu-ally awakened life, they will not settle for less. They will not be fooled by the shining tinsel of a purely materialistic existence. They will want it all—enlight-enment, loving relationships, and meaningful work. Once they are shown the way, they can have it.

• • •

The express route to patience is to go directly to divine remembrance through devotion and meditation. The slower way is the cultivation of the virtues. We can consciously dwell in the higher true Self through divine remembrance or we can work to reduce the self-serving motives of ego—either way is useful and both are even better. The yield is patience with others, with ourselves, with life's unfolding process.

• • •

The Soul's Success

The silence of superconscious meditation is empty of word, sound, or image but full of presence. It resounds with the reality of God within us. Like a crashing wave returns to the ocean's deep peace, dive into the fullness of your boundless existence through the gateway of silence.

• • •

Spiritual detachment requires knowledge of truth and a compassionate heart. Otherwise, it is indifference. Awakened detachment is what the saints have called "caring but not caring." This is freedom from fearing or clinging to any changeable circumstance, all the while caring deeply for what is real.

• • •

Approach the scriptures reverently as you would a loving mother or father, anticipating the wealth of wisdom contained within them to be freely shared with you. To contemplate scripture as a vital source of guidance, read and then inquire within to know its true meaning. Expect revelation. True knowledge always unfolds from within.

• • •

Do good deeds and leave the knowledge of them to God alone. This strengthens our divine connection and weakens ego's hold.

• • •

Love's persistence overcomes despair's insistence that our simple acts of lovingkindness are not sufficient. Once our innate divinity is revealed, we spontaneously act in accordance with it. True revelation purifies heart and mind, and spontaneous goodness—kindness in thought, speech, and action—pours forth like a mountain stream after the snowmelt in spring.

• • •

We can sometimes be too quick to toss something aside or ignore what might be mended or polished. Tenderness and lovingkindness are present in the willingness to repair both things and relationships. One divine energy pervades and enlivens everything. Nothing exists without that essence. Taking care, mending, honoring life in its many forms, we too begin to feel cared for.

• • •

Seek to possess God alone and free yourself from the endless urge to possess everything perceived as enjoyable. When a cloth is fully saturated it cannot absorb more. Be saturated with divine joy.

• • •

Struggle and suffering can be the soul's friends. When they come to visit, they let us know we have forgotten the truth of who we are.

• • •

When trying to discern the right path of service we can ask, *Who does it benefit? What does it promote?* If it is constructive, if it serves the whole, bringing more unity and less divisiveness, more awareness and greater peace, we are moving in the right direction.

• • •

Suppressing emotion is like pressing down on a coiled spring. When conditions are right, it will spring back. Respect emotion. Let it rise in its own time. Gather the wisdom it brings and practice detachment so that it moves gracefully back into its seat, comfortable and quiet.

• • •

What one person sees as an obstacle, another may clearly see as opportunity. We see situations or conditions as obstacles when we are attached to a particular way or outcome. Remove the attachment, replace it with openness and curiosity, and the obstacle vanishes. The sword of discernment transforms it into opportunity.

• • •

To align with life's prospering activity, do not try to prosper. Instead, seek to align.

• • •

Our right work is not a job; our right work is to develop spiritually. What we do in life is the vehicle for becoming, for our soul to express its potential. Instead of asking, *What should I do?* we can ask, *What must I become in order to fulfill my purpose?*

• • •

See things as they are—neither inherently pleasant nor unpleasant. Look within to find the thoughts and beliefs that color your perception. Know that you have the power to see things clearly. With the eye of discernment, see what is so.

• • •

There is no secret to success. Simply go forward with awareness and perseverance. Our path is unknown and unseen, until we walk it. Only our dedicated steps taken in the light of awakened consciousness reveal it.

• • •

Nurture your soul by feasting on truth. Fast from worry, fear, and all forms of negativity and you will grow stronger in spiritual consciousness. Life is ready and willing to give us all that we need in this moment. When we let go of the past, this truth is abundantly revealed.

• • •

Observe the nature of thoughts moving through the mental field. They arise like a wave moving forward with the energy of association and memory. If we ignore a thought, it will rise and then subside. When the wave is spent, we can rest in the conscious calm of the interim before another wave begins. In that calm interval, dive into the deep peace of the Self.

• • •

How do we live in the soul? Respond to the
promptings of conscience.

• • •

Those who practice meditation soon learn that
silence is something much greater than not speaking
words or even the absence of environmental sound.
Once our awareness moves within beyond external
sound, and then beyond the subtle inner noise of
sensation, thought, and feeling, it comes to rest in
the essence of our being. It is there that we discover
true silence. When we rest in the silent awareness of
our spiritual nature, the door of infinite knowledge
and blessing opens to us.

• • •

The seeds planted in this moment are the flowers
of our future. Be mindful of your thoughts and
emotions. They are the seeds that blossom and bear
fruit according to their nature. If we yearn for peace,
we must cultivate it first in our own consciousness.

• • •

In meditation, with eyes closed, lift your gaze above the inner horizon at the third eye center. Seek the inner light of wisdom there as you would wait for the rising sun at dawn.

• • •

Our ability to surrender to God is directly related to mental and emotional maturity, a strong foundation of faith, and steady spiritual practice. Spiritual surrender is not a passive act. It is an active giving over of self-protection and self-will, a vote of confidence in the Infinite, a decision to trust. It is releasing the erroneous idea of a separate self. Surrender can happen in a moment, but living a surrendered life requires practice and daily commitment.

• • •

Cultivate a beginner's mind by practicing nonattachment to views. Adopt a perspective of openness, curiosity, and willingness to discover. Possibilities, like a night filled with thousands of vibrating stars, reveal themselves to an open mind.

• • •

There are two primary paths before us in life: one based in error that disappoints, or leads to sorrow, and one grounded in truth that leads to lasting fulfillment. Learning to discern which is which, and having the willingness and courage to follow the latter is the practice for those who commit to spiritually-conscious living. A spiritual seeker looks at the path of truth and wonders where it will lead. A disciple embarks on that path and follows it with steadfastness, faith, and devotion, ever intent on Self-realization.

• • •

Though the physical teacher may fail or disappoint us, God is always the true teacher. That Divine Presence will continue to make Itself known as the heart remains open. Even the breaking of the heart in the student-teacher relationship can serve this purpose. Only that which is founded in truth and emanates love has lasting value. This is true of all actions, relationships, and teachings.

• • •

Those who have a pure heart and mind bless and uplift others with their thoughts, speech, and actions. Even the thought of such a person brings peace and happiness. Be like that.

• • •

Include the soul's joy in your definition of success.

• • •

Sweep away negative or self-defeating thoughts with a conscious out-breath. Welcome happiness back into your heart and mind with a conscious in-breath. It takes only one transforming moment, one breath.

• • •

Becoming a disciple is not something we do in a moment. We may, in a grace-filled instance, say "yes" to dedicating our life to spiritual awakening. Yet it is living the disciplined life every day and demonstrating the willingness to learn, that is discipleship.

• • •

The heart's deepest desire is a candle within us, ready to be ignited by our willingness to thrive and our decision to live a life that is true to the soul. The commitment to live a life that is worthy of us propels us on the highway of our divine calling and destiny. Risk taking the high road.

• • •

We cannot have the new life that we seek without letting go of the past. Respect the way things are and live in the soul's unconditional joy in the present moment, even in the midst of loss. Real freedom— soul freedom—is not being in control. It is letting go. It is being free of the need to manipulate, to manage, or to map out. Free of false certainty and predictability, life is ever-new.

• • •

Renunciation is not renouncing the world or our duties in it. The abode of the true renunciate is the cave of the heart. Such a person engages in life fully, serves God without seeking recognition, does not cling to desired results of action, and is perpetually free to be happy without a reason.

• • •

Surrendered Devotion

When we are surrendered to God, a change in consciousness is unavoidable. It occurs in our life like the approaching dawn. There is a long time in the dark, then slowly, barely perceptible changes begin to occur until finally the entire landscape of our life is illumined.

• • •

Dwelling on the faults of others is an indication that we are not tending to our own. The only truly effective work we can do is on ourselves. Faultfinding is the result of an overactive, distracted mind. Those who complain about others are motivated by ego, trying to prop themselves up by tearing someone else down. Those intent on spiritual growth sincerely give thanks for the difficult people in their lives. It is true that we often learn the most about ourselves from them. Inwardly acknowledge the inherent goodness of others regardless of their behavior. Look to their strengths and affirm them. Remember that at the core of their being, they are God's perfect expressions. Look for divine harmony in all circumstances. Refuse the mindset of blame by cultivating awareness of what is good and calling it forth. Let the rest fall away.

• • •

Surrender of the sense of separation does not mean extinction of the individual. It means that the activity of the Divine can now flow freely through that individual without the conflict of wills. Sometimes devotees fear what God might ask of them if they surrender. This is because they have not yet discovered that God is already their life.

• • •

Meditation is the vehicle for changing the direction of our lives from self-serving to surrender. This shift in our perspective occurs when we realize that what we are looking for is already within us—profound peace, innate wholeness, and bliss. Surrender is letting go of the struggle to acquire what we already have. When we are surrendered, meditation and prayer occur naturally, regularly, and spontaneously throughout the day. Bliss begets bliss.

• • •

Divine housekeeping tips: Empty the ego trash of resentment, pride, and jealousy. Reuse and recycle love and appreciation. Polish the heart with thoughts of God.

• • •

Compassionate action flows naturally from one who sees the underlying unity of all life with the light of an awakened heart. We know compassion because it is a divine quality that already exists in us. We yearn to experience it more fully because we have tasted it. The sweetness of it is within our own hearts; our conscience speaks of it daily.

• • •

Gratitude comes when we let go. When we cease fighting what is, the glory of what can be emerges. Dwell in gratitude and your mind will be calm, your heart will open, and joy will overflow. "Thank you" is a powerful mantra.

• • •

Make the astounding journey from the head to the heart. This is the way of surrender. It is letting go of the mental conversation about how things need to be different than they are, or thinking that we are somehow separate from God. The spiritual life continually invites us to let go—let go of holding onto the past, let go of trying to become someone, and let go of the illusion that we are separate from the Source. All of that clinging and holding on takes effort. We feel it as stress. When we notice it, we can ask: *what would it be like to just let go?*

• • •

To commit ourselves to following the deeper truth of the spiritual way, we must give up attachment to appearances. We may appear inconsistent, even foolish at times, while we are growing stronger inside. This is profoundly different from someone who is committed to a polished facade while the inside is crumbling.

• • •

Our need for shelter is basic. It occurs on all levels of our being—from the physical need to shelter and care for the body; to the emotional need for loving-kindness, compassion, and forgiveness; to the spiritual need to consciously seek refuge in the Self. When the ego provides shelter, it is like a corrupt landowner who misuses the labor of tenant farmers for his own greed and leaves them with nothing. When we turn to God for shelter, all is given and more.

• • •

Choose your life! Risk following your authentic path to be fully who you are. Even if you fail in your initial attempts, it will still be the right choice. How else do we discover our full potential?

• • •

We align with divine will when we stop asking life to serve us and, instead, commit ourselves to serving life. Those who serve with the intention to help others often discover they have entered a purifying fire in which they, themselves, are transformed. We think we are helping others but soon discover that we are the ones who are lifted up. Divine love does that. Through grace, it opens our eyes, humbles us, welcomes us into the sanctuary of belonging.

• • •

The sense of urgency coming from the ego insists it has to be "my way" and it must be now. The wisdom of the soul, even when prompted to take immediate action, rarely carries the tinge of urgency that is characteristic of self-will. Be suspicious of urgency. When it accompanies desire, it usually belongs to ego and self-will. What is the hurry about?

• • •

Ego is a seamstress working around the clock, sewing our desires together to make a curtain. That curtain, made of attachment to our likes and aversion to our dislikes, blocks our view of the unity of life. Use the tool of Self-knowledge to remove the thread of ignorance and the fabric of illusion will completely unravel.

• • •

To awaken spiritually and thrive in all ways, grace is necessary. A life filled with self-will misses the deeper happiness that comes through being a recipient of God's unlimited grace that is always present. We open ourselves to it through surrender. A heartfelt offering of the simple prayer, "not my will but Thine be done," provides a way. Spiritual surrender not only gives us support, but also offers us delight. Through surrender, we consciously enter God's lila—life's divine play that exists for the sake of joy. We are not separate from that joy, but it takes surrender to realize this.

• • •

When the higher true Self and the small self are not in harmony, confusion naturally results. As vexing as it might be, confusion can become a powerful ally if we stop seeing it as an obstacle and instead become curious about it. If we ask, *Why am I confused?* we likely see the obvious struggle between conflicting choices. But we can mentally step outside of that conflict and confusion and ask different questions, like, *What do I already know about this that I'm afraid to admit?* Or, *What would I do if I wasn't confused at all?*

• • •

Personal desires—all of our likes and dislikes—are the identity constructing materials of the ego. Without attachment to them, ego cannot build its house.

• • •

Insights for serving in joy: At the beginning, offer a prayer of dedication. While working, offer results to the Divine. At the conclusion, offer prayers of gratitude. The joy of service becomes a burden whenever we are attached to the outcome or imagine ourselves as the doer. When we experience the fullness of the soul's joy, it naturally spills over into selfless service and love for all.

• • •

Anger, lust, and greed are the result of misdirected soul force. Instead of following the soul's inspiration, the ego attempts to dominate life though partnership with the senses and desire. But when the senses come under the dominion of the surrendered, soul-inspired ego, anger, lust, and greed lose their jobs and move to the outskirts of the city. If those troublesome emotions resurface, you can surmise that ego has moved back in with desire.

• • •

There are times when we are tempted to fall prey to old belief systems of not having enough, being enough, or thinking that our participation does not matter. These are delusions of the ego asserting its story of being separate from the Source. See it for what it is and let it go. We can often recognize ego when it puts on the outfit of superiority and arrogance. It can be more difficult to spot its seemingly humble guise. Either way, the felt sense of isolation gives it away.

• • •

Prosperous living is based on awareness of the spiritual truth of our being. It is not something that happens in our life when we get what we want nor is it something that we achieve. It is not based on what we have or what we do. It is a way of life. Ask nothing. Want nothing. Give everything you can. These are the keys to wealth beyond measure.

• • •

Inner peace is an attractive environment. It invites inspiration and guidance. Do not be overly involved with mundane thoughts, worries, or things. Refuse to let your mind become disturbed by the ten thousand things that arise. Dive deeper, below the surfaces of things, to find imperturbable peace.

• • •

Inescapable Freedom and Joy

Great souls know nothing of failure. At every turn
of fortune, they see the opportunity to learn.

• • •

One desire alone has the potential to bring prosperity
to all aspects of our life—our deepest yearning to
realize our essential nature. Only that reveals our
innate fullness; nothing external that we add on will
ever suffice.

• • •

A sure sign of spiritual awakening is the
presence of unconditional joy.

• • •

There is no need to look for love; it is not separate
from us. Love, compassion, and kindness are divine
qualities inherent to the soul nature of every person.
The greatest romance is the divine romance. Once
divine love fills our heart and mind, every relationship improves. Love is everywhere to be found,
everywhere to be shared.

• • •

You are free to be happy for no reason.

• • •

Self-knowledge is the shelter for every storm. It brings peace where there is provocation, joy where there is sorrow, and clarity where there was once confusion. Conditions are always changing, but they occur or arise on the ground of being, which is unchanging. Remember who you really are—that changeless Reality.

• • •

We do not have to act on every desire or impulse we have, even those that may be alluring. What will it serve? Observing the way that desire arises, peaks, and then subsides, brings tremendous insight, power, and freedom. We realize we are masters of our energy. Spiritual awareness gives us the great gift of the pause—a conscious moment where we can observe what is arising, inquire into it, and then choose an appropriate response. This is freedom.

• • •

The less distraction we create with our wants, the more peace we discover within us and the more satisfaction we find with what we already have. In a materialistically-oriented culture, the consumer can quickly become consumed by wanting more and more. The ability to experience soul satisfaction frees us from falling into that trap.

• • •

Grief is like an ocean wave that sweeps over the ego taking everything away with it. If we let go into our grief with awareness, without trying to resist or control life, it can take us into the depths of our being where the true Self is revealed.

• • •

Spiritual practice may be intermittent in the beginning. Good habits take time to form. Surround yourself with other devotees of God. In a spiritual community, there is opportunity to learn and to uplift one another by example. The wisdom and divine companionship we experience with such company helps us build faith and strengthen our resolve. With dedication and perseverance, practice becomes steady, an integral part of each day. Like a pilgrim in Mecca circling the Kaaba, Self-realization becomes the center of all we think, say, and do.

• • •

Daily meditation and prayer infuses a home environment like a sweet fragrance. Others notice it. A sense of peace pervades the atmosphere and subtly uplifts those who enter. Our home becomes a holy place.

• • •

Balanced living requires restraint, yet it opens the body and mind to unbounded spiritual energy and freedom. It brings forth an experience of unrestrained aliveness akin to standing in a vast open meadow in full bloom teeming with new life.

• • •

When our relationship to the senses is transformed through meditation and nonattachment, the senses become instruments for detecting God's infinite beauty and grace everywhere. There is no need, or reason, to negate the senses and sensory experience. Who would want to do that? Once purified through spiritual awakening, eyes become mirrors that reflect God in all; ears hear the divine song reverberating throughout the universe; the nose detects the sweet fragrance of flowers offering devotion to the One; hands touch the pulse of presence everywhere; and the tongue tastes the honey of divine remembrance.

• • •

True worship is to realize God by actualizing the divine qualities of discernment, compassion, and justice—to refuse to compromise our self, to do what we know we should do, what our heart says *yes* to, what we know is right.

• • •

When we free ourselves from the idea that anything actually belongs to us and from the illusion that we can completely control outcomes, we free ourselves from stress. Cultivate nonattachment, the great stress-reducer.

• • •

When we consciously choose to serve God with our work, it becomes transforming. It is lifted from the mundane to the miraculous in small or great ways. We may stay with the same line of work consistently, or we may change jobs. Either way, we, and the work we do, will keep growing and transforming. No matter what we do, we can hold this higher vision and intention. It illumines the way of skillful means, reveals dharmic choices, and intuitive insights that support us in our journey of spiritual awakening.

• • •

When thoughts settle in meditation, we naturally experience inner peace. Be conscious of that experience and take it in. Notice it and feel your awareness expand into it. You can take it with you wherever you go. Here's how: After meditating, take a few minutes to inwardly "gather up" that peace and intend to share it with everyone you meet.

• • •

Do we work for security, prosperity, or happiness? It is true that work can offer all of that. It can also offer insecurity, fear of lack, and unhappiness. If we imagine our job as the source of our happiness or unhappiness, security or lack of it, we have missed the deeper truth. Realizing that enduring happiness, security, and prosperity are soul qualities, allows us to more fully appreciate the various channels for experiencing that in the world. We do not need to confuse the channel with the source. We can always change the channel.

• • •

When you meditate and visit the ocean of divine bliss, why just stand upon the shore? Dive in. Dive into the soul! Immerse yourself in the luminous radiance of the Self. Peace will greet you and joy will attend to your every need.

• • •

The spiritual teacher provides a map for the path of awakening. The teachings, when embraced with faith and practiced by the devotee, are the connecting link between guru and disciple, or spiritual teacher and student. The student must make the journey and live the teachings. The ticket for enlightenment is not transferable.

• • •

The benefits of daily meditation touch all areas of our life. As awareness grows, we experience radiant health, a peaceful mind, and harmonious relationships. Draw a circle of unbroken awareness from your meditation seat to every action in your day. Know that you are the conscious witness of your thoughts and actions. Remain inwardly serene and unmoved by changing conditions. Return to your Self again and again.

• • •

Like a serene lake reflecting the light of the full moon on a clear night, the quiet mind is capable of revealing our essential Self—pure existence-being, unmoving, unchanging, eternal Spirit.

• • •

A disciple undergoes the essential transformation of heart and mind in order to progress from being a seeker of the way to one who embodies the way.

• • •

Spiritual discipleship heralds a simple but profound change in our orientation towards life. It is simple: we become teachable. It is profound: we possess the necessary receptivity to embrace our soul's destiny. We are ready to live our eternal life.

• • •

To offer love and appreciation in all that we do is to express our higher nature. Offering unconditional love is recognizing a mutual aliveness, a shared reality in God. Admiring a little bird, or a flower, can be an offering of love if we see God, and not just an object.

• • •

Once discernment reveals ego's fallibility, an opening occurs for true Self-knowledge to be revealed. When the mental field is purified, free from ego's shadow of illusion, the light of the Self pervades the mind. What we are then shines through, unmistakably.

• • •

The spiritually-dedicated life is one where we wrestle, like Jacob with the angel, to receive the blessing in all that is and bring it forth. We actively participate in our own destiny and that of our awakening world. We are not alone. The Divine Presence responds to our need and comes in a time of darkness and despair with saving grace. This grace reveals the way of awakening from darkness to light, ignorance to bliss, bondage to freedom. Be a spiritual warrior. If you are struggling with a situation, take charge, turn it around. Demand a blessing instead.

• • •

Kindness is contagious.

• • •

Once God is found in the temple of our hearts, we find the divine radiance everywhere. We see the One shining in all eyes, and hear the divine name resounding in every sound—the song of a bird, the ringing of a phone, even the subtle humming of our own breath.

• • •

A great self-confidence begins to bloom in us when we experience our true nature as one with the Source. Released from old fears and debilitating habits, we can now engage in life fully. True self-confidence is confidence in the Self.

• • •

Spiritual friendship is based primarily on shared values. Shared interests are secondary. As spiritual awakening progresses, some friendships deepen, while others fall away. Appreciate all, and let it be.

• • •

Transform relationships by relating soul to soul. Without words, simply acknowledge the presence of God within everyone. Watch what happens.

• • •

In superconscious meditation, dwell in silence
and drink from the holy well.

• • •

Intellectual knowledge is useful in many areas of life,
but has limits when it comes to spiritual realization.
Even accurate information will not dispel spiritual
ignorance—the lack of true Self knowledge or the
difficulty it brings. Ignorance flees from accurate
knowledge combined with the direct perception of
truth—this is spiritual realization. When we have
direct perception of truth and begin to live it—this
is wisdom. With spiritual wisdom lasting happiness
is possible.

• • •

When we enter the temple we experience peace
because our own inner peace is revealed to us as we
become quiet and receptive. The attitude of worship,
which is reverence and receptivity, builds temples
wherever we go.

• • •

What makes your soul sing with joy? Discover that.
When we know inner joy, discipline is easy. Our goals
are met as a natural out-picturing of a contented
heart and mind.

• • •

The True Self
is Unseen

We are on earth but a little while. The real reason for being here is very different from what most people imagine. There is a fundamental purpose for our lives. To know it, we must know life's origin and where it is going, look beyond our short-term goals to what we ultimately want to accomplish, and consider life's highest potential for development.

—Paramahansa Yogananda

We Are Already Free

Sometimes life can break your heart—no one escapes its sorrows. Yet in the midst of every sorrow is the persistent rising sun of truth, illuminating every situation with the light of "I am That." Beyond any circumstance, deeper than any pain or sorrow, the blessed Self shines through proclaiming, "Arise, awake."

• • •

The stream of spiritual transformation often flows underground as we are being remade in the depths of our being and a change of heart is underway. We may sense only darkness on the surface, an aridity that challenges our faith. Consider that at such times we are being shaped by the unseen divine Self and enlarged in trust. Even in times of great darkness, grace is at work in a surrendered heart.

• • •

Our best friend is our higher Self. To be a friend to that Self requires the discipline of turning within, becoming aware of our deepest desire to live a holy life, and doing it. Be confident in your Self. Go forth boldly; do that which is yours to do.

• • •

Countless side paths beckon every day. Getting caught up with others is a diversion from our own path of Self-realization. Keep turning your heart and mind to God and walk ahead with wisdom and compassion. Refuse to be distracted by what others say or do. Let them be.

• • •

If we do not see the suffering that results from unconscious living, there is little motivation for finding freedom. The desire to live an ethical life is necessary preparation for liberation. To get beyond our fears and prejudices we must first admit we have them, then recognize them as thoughts and beliefs we can change. We can choose a higher path whenever we are ready. All the supportive powers of Nature and the presence of divine grace are waiting.

• • •

When we meditate and our attention wanders away from our focus and is then recollected, we have a choice. We can bemoan our distracted state of mind, or be curious about what called us back. The former leads to a flurry of dissatisfaction, the latter to deepening insight.

• • •

Who is this "I" that claims ownership? A thief, that is all. Ego is the CEO of the advertising firm of "I, Me, and Mine." It continually creates desires to maintain the illusion that we need what it is selling us—happiness from having this or attaining that, or security from achieving this or owning that. Ego says, "My house, my car, my husband or wife, my child, my body." In truth, none of this actually belongs to us. All of it is simply on loan, including our bodies. Remember God is our larger true life. The happiness, wholeness, and well-being we desire are innate. They reside in the true Self. Be free of the "I" that would separate you from the Source by using the boundary of "me and mine." Without clinging to desires, the ego starts to crumble. What remains when desires and attachments are removed is the "I Am"—conscious existence Itself.

• • •

Attempting to arrange outer conditions to sustain happiness takes us far from the source of true happiness within us. While the ego uses life energy on expedition after expedition, the soul life languishes. If the mind, free of the strivings of the false self, sinks into the heart of divine remembrance, an incomparable joy arises within us.

• • •

The first support for dealing with obstacles is to anticipate them. Anticipate and expect that life will present opportunities as part of the growth process leading to our greater good. When you encounter an obstacle, consider that it is only an obstacle because you allow it to be one. Inquire, *What can I let go of that would transform this situation?* We can always transform an obstacle into an opportunity for creative insight when we approach it with the confidence that higher guidance will come.

• • •

Suffering can result from believing the stories we tell ourselves about the way things are. Our thoughts and the stories they weave are a product of the mind. They give us only a partial view of life, not the bigger picture. Step out of the story and see.

• • •

Indulging in moods is a great cause of unhappiness that hurts us and others, too. Remember that you are the soul with the power to resist and overcome any mood. With soul power, open your mind to contentment. It is available to you in this moment. Call it forth and claim it.

• • •

Be yourself without worry. A worried mind is preoc-
cupied with thoughts of the future. A despairing
mind returns again and again to the past. Awareness
of our essential spiritual nature requires us to bring
our attention into the present moment. Only in the
pure present—not one instant before or after—can
we experience freedom from want. Throughout the
day, practice returning attention and awareness to
the present moment. Look beyond what you see with
your eyes and peer into the day with a clear mind and
an awakened heart. Enter the day as a child ready to
play and wonder in the shining moment.

• • •

No amount of self-control or discipline will create
joy, or love, or peace because they are divine qualities.
They are not the result of something we do or produce.
These qualities of the soul cannot be purchased, won,
or acquired. As divine qualities, they are revealed; they
flower from within us when conditions are right. The
only way to reap joy, love, and peace is to welcome
them now and allow them to come forth.

• • •

How can we move from injury to forgiveness? From sadness to joy? From being hurt to being healed? Standing on one side looking over at the other, it seems like an abyss that we cannot possibly cross. Only when we actually take the leap do we discover that we can. The abyss is surrender. The jump is letting go of self-will. The moment we stop clinging to self-will and surrender to our Higher Power, we become teachable. This is a moment that changes us forever.

• • •

The idea that another person can make us whole, or bring us fulfillment, is inaccurate. Imagining we are less than we really are takes away from a relationship. Bringing awareness of our wholeness to a relationship enriches it. Two people, each aware of their own innate fullness, can enjoy a creative, wholesome, loving, intimate relationship. Free of false dependency, neither needs to try to possess or manipulate the other. When fullness is realized in relationship, love overflows.

• • •

The secret of secrets is not revealed to anyone whose heart is hardened by self-hatred or contempt for the spiritual life. To access inner wisdom and receive the teachings of the higher Self, our heart must open. To be pure in heart is to be completely open, utterly transparent to the inner light of the Self.

• • •

Work, duties, and responsibilities are not an interference to spiritual awakening. They are essential to it, offering a mirror for us to see our growing edge. How else to recognize such hindrances as jealousy, anger, or selfishness that otherwise remain hidden from view? Those who are intent on awakening enter the world of action rejoicing.

• • •

When old ways of being die out, the opportunity for spiritual transformation is upon us. Nothing is more practical than spiritual realization and nothing transforms our lives for better in such a complete way. We yearn for this transformation, yet it can be daunting to be free, to live in a new way without old coping mechanisms, the false friends of bad habits. Recognize fear of this change as the feeling of your life sprouting wings.

• • •

What difference does it make to recognize the innate power of the soul? It brings us the gift of understanding that we have the power within us to be free. The power to be happy. The power to know whatever we desire to know.

• • •

The quickest way to lose inner peace is to argue with the way things are. The quickest way to regain it is to accept what is. True peace is a quality of our divine nature that is great enough to contain and transform any conflict.

• • •

We may think that outer circumstances cause our experiences. It can be useful to consider the possibility that our own tendencies have drawn us to particular circumstances. One who understands this is close to freedom.

• • •

Some people spend their entire lives focused on changing others when the only real power we have is to change ourselves. We discover inner peace when we stop trying to make others, circumstances, or the world conform to our desires.

• • •

Sometimes we wonder: How we can possibly give time to spiritual practice when our days are already full? Sages of all traditions throughout time have offered the same message: if we put realization of Truth at the center of our life, everything else comes to us with grace and ease. Living consciously with spiritual focus and priorities is the best time management strategy of all.

• • •

Our body and mind are influenced by the tendencies in nature. The tendency of inertia leads us to indulge the senses—to overeat and oversleep until we are weighed down with heaviness. The tendency of restlessness leads us to constantly seek activity and success while it clouds our deeper power and insight. The elevating tendency fosters equanimity and contentment and leads us to peace. The mind, influenced by the first two tendencies and allowed to roam wherever it will, at first resists the discipline of meditation. Meditation is the natural environment for the elevating, illuminating tendency to flourish. Its discipline is joy.

• • •

Go Straight to the Goal

When our life is out of balance—too much food, sleep, action, or inaction—the body and mind become occupied with attempting to regain equilibrium. Balance releases the energy necessary to focus dynamically and achieve success. With focus and dedication, balance is restored and inner peace is attained.

• • •

Accept others as they are. If you are complaining about others, you have lost contact with your higher true Self. Regain your center and everyone will improve. What is the use of fault-finding, of criticizing and blaming others or even God? It is a disease of the mind that infects everyone around us. Appreciation is the cure.

• • •

It is easy to believe we are even-minded—non-reactive to praise or blame—when we are showered with praise. Our ability to learn from the heat of criticism is more telling.

• • •

We imagine freedom to be the ability to choose what we like over what we dislike or to have what we want and avoid what we do not want. This can be deceptive, a kind of sugarcoated bondage. The highest freedom is release from being compelled by either likes or dislikes, attractions or aversions. Spiritual insight, revealing the nature of desire, shows us a natural way to approach our choices—reduce strong desires to lightly held preferences. This is the way to free ourselves from grasping.

• • •

Only a thief enjoys the abundant gifts of God without serving others in return. Eventually such a thief is locked up in the prison of self. True generosity is liberating. Even a thief can learn from this.

• • •

Our way of working can either delight or burden us. Work itself does not cause the feeling of being overwhelmed. Our experience can be traced to the thoughts we bring, the messages we give ourselves and others about it, and the stories we tell. Cultivating delight in our work right where we are helps us grow clearer and stronger about what is ours to do. If our workplace is not right, we will gracefully move on to another.

• • •

Sensory attraction to objects of desire is like a creeping vine. At first the desire blossoms and the object is alluring. But when the vine grows unrestrained, it eventually covers the entire garden, even making the house inaccessible. We are so used to moving from the fulfillment of one desire to the next that it seems nearly impossible to imagine a life free from chasing after externals. But this is an excellent place to begin. Imagine what it would be like to be free of clinging to what you want, free to live in the spontaneous flow of what is.

• • •

Reading too much without contemplation and putting into practice; eating too much without mindful awareness, good digestion, and exercise; and talking too much without listening, are forms of greed. Identifying and naming such behaviors for what they are at the root is a first step towards lessening their influence. When negative human tendencies such as greed, lust, jealousy, and hatred are decreased, the happiness and contentment of the soul begins to weave itself throughout our experience.

• • •

In our active lives with multiple demands, the needs of the soul for solitude, meditation, and contemplation seem the easiest to ignore. Those who thrive in all areas of life know that honoring the soul must come first. This sets the tone for everything else we do. It is not enough to say we know the soul life is important; we must honor it daily. If we think of our daily meditation practice as one more thing to do, it will be dry, hurried, and unsatisfactory. Recognize it as your time to saturate yourself with bliss and open yourself to divine wisdom and power. You will be abundantly fueled for the day ahead.

• • •

The need to always be right is a refusal to grow. Becoming aware of our mistakes can strike a painful blow to the ego. But being able to admit our mistakes allows us to correct more than the error. It opens the door to repentance and improvement of character. If our goal is spiritual transformation, it becomes possible to rejoice in the opportunity for growth that such awareness brings.

• • •

Impatience, frustration, and irritability are all shades of anger related to thwarted desire. If we practice imperturbability and keep our composure, we short-circuit the karmic trap by freeing ourselves from present pain and future unhappiness.

• • •

The only thing that stops us from experiencing divine love is us—our thoughts about who we are.

• • •

Attachment to the results of our actions binds us to time. When there is desire for the fruit of action, the mind travels between the present moment and the imagined future. Work with integrity now and let the rest unfold in divine order. By trying to grasp future good fortune, we lose touch with the opportunity of this moment.

• • •

Sometimes we hold on so tight to what we want, or think is right, that we cannot see the divine possibilities before us. Only when we are completely willing—to stay or to go, to have or not have, to discover something entirely new—only then does higher guidance make itself known to us.

• • •

Whenever you are inclined to talk about lack, remember that from the spiritual perspective of infinite being and power, lack is an illusion. It is a temporary condition, something that is always subject to change. Transform that moment of forgetting the Source into an opportunity to remember omnipresent divine support instead.

• • •

Both good and bad habits are the children of our thought process. We bring them into being and support them with attention and repeated action. Then we become convinced they are a part of us we cannot do without. We can change any habit when we see how we created it. Erroneous thinking can be released through discernment. In any moment, we can return to awareness of our essential Self which is ever-conscious, ever-free. However, we may need to repeat this adjustment in many conscious moments. This is spiritual practice. This is sadhana, going straight for the goal.

• • •

Human behavior can be strange. We have an experience and then we analyze it. We make a decision about that experience and what it means. We tell ourselves and others the story about it. Then we start to live out of that decision as if it were reality itself. When we discern the distinction between that which changes, and Absolute Reality which is unchanging, such stories lose their power to unduly influence us.

• • •

Renounce any false ideas and attachments to people, circumstances, or things as the source of your happiness. Where there is attachment there will ultimately be anger, disappointment, resentment, and all their unpleasant relatives who come to visit. Do not entertain them or they will stay with you. Embrace the exhilaration that comes with letting go.

• • •

Restless desire—wanting what we want when we want it, or striving for results—is a great contributor to stress. When we are caught up in it, it seems we only need to work harder to get the desired results. What if we actually need to do less? Less doing, less pushing, and instead, more letting go and being fully present?

• • •

Keep the mind focused throughout the day on thoughts of God, or the name of God, and find refuge from worries and fear. God is the sheltering power—the source of all good, protection, and peace. Take shelter in That. Troubles come and go; they are insubstantial. Look past them to the One.

• • •

All of life is energy. Our thoughts and actions can either lead toward freedom that liberates us from sorrow, or toward involvement that brings suffering. With our every thought, word, and action, we move energy toward manifestation. Once we understand this spiritual law, we can be increasingly aware of the subtle influences we are setting in motion by noticing the intentions behind our thoughts, words, and actions. Do they intend to bless, uplift, encourage, or help? Or, do they destroy, tear down, discourage, or degrade? Even the smallest act done with a pure heart filled with divine love, blossoms, bears fruit, and becomes nourishment for all.

• • •

Tend Your Soul Fire

Cultivate love, offer service, and light the lamps of devotion. These qualities raise our consciousness from the horizon of ego's limitations to the infinite sky of divine Truth.

• • •

The influence of environment is powerful. We are wise to consider it. Although our essence of being is untouched by any environment, as a practical matter we seek out those environments that are most supportive of our total well-being. Especially when we are establishing new, healthy habits, it is important to pay attention to what we surround ourselves with. Habits are triggered by environment. If we are tired, stressed, or otherwise off balance, we are likely to respond to those things that trigger lack of self-care, or forgetfulness of ourselves as divine beings. Even if we had previously intended to behave differently, the old coping mechanisms return. To succeed, arrange an environment conducive to success and spiritual remembrance. Keep it simple, keep it sweet.

• • •

We cannot create, acquire, or earn a spiritual condition. Trying to be spiritual is based on a false premise. Don't worry about being spiritual. Let go of trying to get there; instead know you have arrived. Be authentic. Greet your Self with reverence.

• • •

A true friend is one who nurtures our soul into full expression. Some people try to hold others back and imagine that secures their own position. Yet truth cannot be suppressed. Seek the company of those who lift your spirit—true friends. When we commit to our own enlightenment and to the enlightenment of others, it enhances every relationship.

• • •

To live powerfully, focus. So often we move through the day in a distracted state—doing one thing physically while the mind wanders elsewhere. That dissipates our soul power. Focusing our attention gathers soul power like a magnifying glass captures the rays of the sun and lights a fire.

• • •

Breath, time, food, vital force, and money—all are expressions of our life force. To live well, pay attention to how you use these five forms of energy.

• • •

Gossip may seem harmless, yet the words we speak put energy into motion. Being awake is being mindful of the effect of our words before we speak and of the consequences of our actions before we take them. There is no such thing as casual speech, only words of power. Every utterance can be constructive; every word can bless.

• • •

Every lie tears the fabric of wholeness and ultimately robs us of our dignity. To be truthful is not always easy, but it is always the road to self-worth and power.

• • •

Turn the ship of your life toward the deeper waters of Self- and God-realization through intentional practice of superconscious meditation. Beyond the crashing waves of ordinary thoughts is a vast sea of luminous peace. In that serene calm, revelation of the true Self awaits.

• • •

Daily conscious contact with God through meditation brings clarity and opens the inner channels of divine guidance. We can then move through all situations with the added blessing of inner assurance.

• • •

Praise and blame are pairs that constantly anticipate one another. Give neither any attention. True self-esteem does not depend on gaining praise or avoiding blame. The accurate sense of self-value is revealed within when we are Self-knowing.

• • •

Conscious eating can be a sacramental occasion when food is recognized as a divine gift to sustain our body temple. The energy of the body, fueled by healthy food, is then given back to God in selfless service. Conscious eating includes the food itself, awareness of how it was grown and prepared, the amount that we eat, and the way we eat it. We mindfully consider the sacrifices that brought the food to us. Everything and everyone is connected. Partake prayerfully and everyone benefits. Moderation in eating is an essential part of this. Food affects the mind and colors our life experience. By noticing that connection, we can take charge of our life. Eat enough healthy food to nourish the body and no more. Healthy restraint brings the same joy as indulgence. Only it is subtler, lasts longer, and has greater far-reaching benefits.

• • •

If we are hurt by criticism, we can deduce that we are also seduced by praise. Both praise and blame can be practice prompters for us, an opportunity for self-inquiry. With praise, inwardly release attachment and give thanks to God for all gifts worthy of praise. In times of blame or criticism, ask if there is any truth in it. If so, use it as an opportunity to grow.

• • •

Beyond what we say or do, it is ultimately our consciousness that others experience. The consciousness of those who are spiritually awake shines like the sun, giving light and warmth to all. Their presence emanates blessing and their words have power. Being near them is an uplifting reminder of our true nature.

• • •

The self-discipline of restraining our appetites and transmuting them toward spiritual focus is like building a hot fire into which we place all of our conditioned ways of being. The heat from this fire gives off tremendous energy that can be used for higher purposes.

• • •

When we desire something so strongly that we are not willing to pause and be still in order to ask for guidance, we set the stage for rampant self-will and the errors and difficulties that surely follow. Self-will is a function of ego that seeks to override our higher wisdom. What could be so important or urgent that we think we cannot stop, even for a moment?

• • •

Just as one thorn may be used to remove another embedded in our foot, we use desire itself to remove those desires that are not useful to our higher purpose. The ardent desire for spiritual awakening can be the thorn that dislodges the painful thorns of distraction and forgetfulness of our true Self.

• • •

While you may initially use some technique to quiet your thoughts when you sit to meditate, let go of it once the mental field becomes calm. Then what? Be curious. Be patient. Look within and listen within. Notice what you experience. Be the conscious witness.

• • •

Enlightenment teachings diagnose ignorance of truth as the cause of all suffering, a disease of the mind. Right spiritual practice is the medicine that supports the cure. Like any medicine, it works only if we take it and follow the prescription for its proper use. Over time, right practice can purify the mind. When the mind is clarified, knowledge of the Self arises that banishes ignorance forever.

• • •

Pride, arrogance, and fear work together to convince us that our life depends on our efforts. Our life depends on God. Change your attitude from "willful" to "will flow" and watch what happens. One is full of self and effort and the other is a joyous letting go.

• • •

We can put a lot of time and energy into trying to get what we want. However, more time sincerely spent in prayer and meditation increases the light or reflection of divinity within our character. This light has a magnetism that draws to it whatever is needed. Consider taking this highway of accomplishment. It is enjoyable and surprisingly more productive.

• • •

Offer God an unwavering mind. If that is not possible, offer a willing heart.

• • •

However formidable an obstacle may appear, from the spiritual perspective the operant word is *appear*. At the heart of our ability to get beyond obstacles is our understanding that divine resources are always available to meet real needs. Cultivate a grateful heart and bring forth what is needed in the present moment from the wealth of divine inspiration within you.

• • •

Work can be an anxiety-producing burden if our motives are strictly self-serving. When our work is consecrated as selfless service and dedicated to a higher purpose, our focus changes. Grace clears away all burdens like blackbirds emptying out of a tree, revealing its green and leafy open arms.

• • •

Resentment builds a prison, thought by thought. Forgiveness tears it down at once. Remove anger and its cousins—resentment, frustration, pride and self-righteousness—from your heart by making it a home for forgiveness instead.

• • •

Sometimes when things go wrong we look for who is to blame. It is useful to distinguish between blame and accountability. To be responsible for our own actions and willing to hold others accountable for theirs is necessary. That can be done with clarity and compassion. Blame is different. It is tinged with anger and is a product of forgetfulness. If we blame others, we have forgotten that we are responsible for our own experience. Everyone and everything is interconnected. When we judge others we also condemn ourselves. Serenity becomes impossible. We can be firm where accountability is concerned and yielding where compassion is needed.

• • •

Fear and restlessness block our conscious entry to the holy present. When we are caught up with how we think life should be rather than how it is, we lose the opportunity for the divine communion of that moment. Anchor your mind in the awareness of God's omnipresence. Fear is removed as the light of unity appears.

• • •

With meditation we learn how to observe our wandering thoughts, how to focus our attention on one point, and how to open our mind to inspiration beyond thought. To live fully and live well, we do the same thing with thoughts and actions during the day. We take this discipline of meditation with us. It is a way that we say to ourselves, *My day begins in God. I live in the constant awareness of that divine Reality throughout my day.* If we do not make time for that divine beginning, how can we expect to be tuned into divine guidance, inspiration, and support throughout the day ahead?

• • •

See Through Appearances

If we see our life as full of problems, it will be. When we look for what is wrong, we find it everywhere. Worry stirs up the mind and blocks our access to inner peace. It obscures discernment, our lighted path to right action. When worry arises, acknowledge the concern and then bring forth the self-care that will restore balance and inner peace. Wait until the mind clears again. Then look. Then see.

• • •

Do what is truly worthwhile. Why chain yourself to insignificant tasks and carry them around with you, the pull of them holding you back? The chains that feel so heavy are the weight of habit. It is a paper chain made by a child—cut it!

• • •

When we believe there is not enough and we strive to get more, we get more of not enough. A change in consciousness—from lack to abundance is needed. To cultivate prosperity consciousness, we can inwardly offer to others what we would most like to have—happiness, love, security. See everyone abundantly blessed.

• • •

Refusing to forgive binds us to the past through aversion. Sometimes people are afraid to forgive because they want to protect themselves against such a hurt ever happening again. They keep resentment alive because they do not want to forget about what happened. But changing our thought patterns from resentment to forgiveness does not give us amnesia. We do not forget what happened; we become better equipped to deal with it with a loving heart and a calm mind. Forgiveness is a change of heart that ultimately occurs through the activity of grace. We cannot immediately change what we deeply feel but we can change our mind. We change our mind through cultivating the willingness to forgive. That is the first step. When grace brings forgiveness in its right time, it frees us, makes us wiser, and expands our capacity to love.

• • •

Gratitude emerges with the discipline of letting go. When we cease fighting with what is, the glory of what can be becomes apparent.

• • •

Offering criticism can be seductive when it masquerades as an attempt to help. Consider the energy it takes to criticize and the effect it has on the spirit of both parties. Real help lifts the spirits of everyone involved.

• • •

When the thinking mind is agitated with worry and fear, the darkness of ignorance clouds our wisdom. This is when discernment is needed. Like a sheriff breaking up a fight, discernment asks the participants to quietly step outside. Stepping into the light, a new perspective emerges. We can similarly step outside our challenges by setting aside our worries and calling on the spiritual power of clear discernment.

• • •

The undisciplined will is like a mischievous puppy that grows into an unmanageable dog that destroys things in the house and the yard. If the same puppy is trained, it could become a guide dog, providing great service to its owner. The destructive energy of self-will can be turned over to divine-will and a pathway for dynamic, inspired living opened up.

• • •

Silent communion with God beyond words and thoughts provides the answer to every prayer. As we emerge from the limits of ego-based consciousness into the infinite allness of our divine nature, every need is met.

• • •

If worry haunts you ask: *Is this thing that worries me true now?* A worried mind lives in an imaginary future. An unhappy mind lives in the storied past. Only a peaceful mind abides in the grace-filled present. In the light of the present, worries flee like a mirage in the hot desert.

• • •

When we have a troubled mind or a physical challenge, it is helpful to pray until we feel the peace of Divine Presence within. In that experience is the assurance that all needs are met, all healing is accomplished, and everything is in divine order. Whenever we experience the truth of this, we have prayed our way through the condition. In that moment we are consciously restored to our original wholeness.

• • •

Spiritual practice is choosing peace, clarity, and compassion in thought, speech, and action. We have only to observe our thoughts and choices to determine whether we are aligning ourselves with peace, chasing after desires, or succumbing to depression or inertia. Practice is making any corrections needed to stay the course of an uplifting way of life. Like a pilot steering toward a chosen destination, constant course correction is necessary until we arrive.

• • •

The quickest way to get out of struggling or unhappiness and enter the flow of immediate blessings is to begin to praise. Affirm, *I am so grateful.* Fill the mind with the light of appreciation and the darkness of negativity will flee.

• • •

It is a common error to think that spiritual awakening will improve our life. It does, but not the way we imagine it will. Often, we are looking for an upgrade—a better version of the way we currently live. Spiritual awakening does not just bring an improved condition; it transforms our consciousness. This is a completely new operating system.

• • •

Prayer turns work into worship.

• • •

The spiritual practice for meeting challenges whether small daily irritations, disappointments, or great difficulties, is the same—to let our thoughts settle. We release moods or worries, regrets and fears, and reconnect to the divine Reality right where we are. Peace comes. Guidance will be revealed. Just wait.

• • •

Suspending the driver's license of the senses takes courage. We become used to the familiar places they take us and imagine we will suffer if we do not follow their lead. But when the soul leads the journey, the senses follow along. New vistas of freedom and joy open before us.

• • •

When things do not go our way the ego wants to curse but the soul recognizes an opportunity to bless. Train your mind to look for the good, to look for truth, and for possibility. The essential spiritual law is: Hold to the One. Seek only Truth. See God in all that is. Doing this, we can recognize the angels of opportunity that begin gathering on our doorstep.

• • •

We have hundreds of choices every day about what we will put our attention on, what thoughts we will cultivate and believe, and what we will allow to influence us. Spiritually-conscious living involves turning—turning away from appearances to rely on what is true, turning away from limiting beliefs and turning toward freedom, turning away from fear and returning to wholeness. It takes boldness to turn and embrace our divine identity but when we do, we discover a beautiful life, overflowing with divine love and grace. Turning toward Truth is the direct path; no preparation is needed.

• • •

Selfless service is not measured by activity. The hallmark of selfless service is the peace and harmony of unity consciousness. This does not come from either activity or inactivity but relies on a pure intent.

• • •

Trying to dissipate anger by venting it is like blowing dandelion seeds in the wind. They will take root and spring up again. Look to the root of anger to find the desire it springs from. Use the trowel of discrimination and pull out the root.

• • •

The world is an opportune place for spiritual realization and the fulfillment that accompanies it. No matter what your current circumstances, consider that there is no other time or place that would be a better support for enlightenment.

• • •

Set yourself free to flourish by focusing on freedom instead of on attachments or aversions—what you want to acquire or hope to avoid. A commitment to spiritual liberation is a commitment to fully realize our innate potential. Freedom can be our compass; it will indicate the direction for finding true success.

• • •

The first step toward spiritual freedom is learning to control restless desires by redirecting our attention to what is useful. True freedom is supported by self-restraint. This is the ability to live in the soul—to choose thoughts, speech and actions that contribute to well-being. On the spiritual path, self-discipline is doing what is in harmony with the soul. Think of it as doing what pleases your soul. With this perspective, discipline is infused with the sweetness of divine love.

• • •

Karma yoga, the path of selfless service, welcomes obstacles and so-called failures as useful resources toward the goal of awakening. Whatever causes us to examine our actions and our motives, and prods us to become more awake and aware, is valuable. The value is not in the doing, that is only the vehicle. The value lies in becoming—what we become as we serve selflessly.

• • •

Bring whatever troubles you have into the awareness of divine order underlying all appearances. Be observant of moods, not mastered by them. Be guided by the steady lamp of truth, not by flashes of emotion or intellectual opinion. Let your awareness be infused completely with truth, the light of Reality. This light breaks through all conditions and reveals their insubstantial nature.

• • •

Habits that are no longer useful flee in the light of clear intention, a viable plan, and positive action. Changing habits is not difficult when the decision to change is backed up by discipline.

• • •

Ignorance of our true nature is the root of all power struggles. Attachment to a particular point of view breeds conflict. Peace returns whenever we remember that we are greater than any viewpoint. Return to your Self; occupy a greater space of awareness where conflicting viewpoints can sit side by side. With that expanded consciousness, we can easily let go of trying to be right and experience peace instead. New insight will come, something fresh. Light from the Self will illumine the way forward.

• • •

Faith provides a point of reference that makes it possible for us to walk through the world and not sink down under the burden of its sorrows. We are aware of them. We experience them with a compassionate heart and an awakened mind. Yet even great sorrows are seen for what they are—boisterous storms that howl one day and clear the next. With God as our constant companion, we can walk in confidence through the wildest of storms.

• • •

Physical actions, creative use of our imagination, and setting intentions are the manifesting tools of the physical, mental, and subtle aspects of our being. One who focuses solely on the physical plane works harder, without the benefit of the power tools of the subtle realms and understanding the laws of cause and effect. When we work first in consciousness, our awareness shifts from outer effect to inner cause. Then there is no struggle to accomplish.

• • •

When we are confronted with difficulty, our thoughts can spin and tension grips the body. First aid for the troubled mind and fearful heart is to attend to the breath. It is the most accessible and reliable way to become still. Simply noticing inhalation and exhalation with the intention to become more inwardly aware restores our equilibrium. Then we can enter the temple of silence in meditation. Even a few moments of meditation strengthens our resilience. We can bend without breaking, move through challenges with clarity and compassion.

• • •

The fire of self-discipline burns away the dross of lethargy and indulgence. It strengthens character and reveals our shining, innate, divine qualities.

• • •

Meditation requires commitment and steadfast attention. Return attention again and again to the focus of meditation, until at last, the peaceful state prevails. Then, let go of any techniques or effort. Just be.

• • •

Who would guess that a brilliant diamond hides in carbon or that rubies are found in a dark cave of plain stone? When we yearn to bring forth healing, the first place to look is within. The way to the peace, security, and well-being we yearn for is within our consciousness. The resources needed are hidden in the cave our own hearts.

• • •

Our Certain Destiny to Awaken

There comes a time in our life when we arrive at the junction of grace and surrender. This is the time when the teacher appears.

• • •

Self-confidence grows as we learn to harness our will power. The more we exercise our wisdom-guided will, the more connected we feel to the soul and its joy.

• • •

To improve relationships, see the best in others. Wish for them the highest good, see them prospering in all ways, and celebrate their successes. Why focus on shortcomings or mistakes, or try to establish blame when mistakes occur? Instead, inwardly affirm that every person is divinely supported and innately whole.

• • •

If we identify with the personality, we are more prone to think we need something that will improve us or make us okay. With spiritual awareness, we still engage in helpful activities that improve our skills or our situation in life. However, we do not mistake what we have or do with what we are.

• • •

Solitude is a friend to the soul.

• • •

Without discipline we cannot find balance. If you learned to ride a bicycle, you will remember the need for constant correction to find balance and not fall off. The spiritual path also requires that initial effort to find our center point and then minor recalibration to stay balanced. As we correct our thoughts, speech, and actions to conform with truth, balance is established. Then the ride is effortless.

• • •

Beyond the honeymoon phase of spiritual practice, there is the hard work of self-examination and self-discipline. But like a fierce storm, the struggle passes. Practice becomes natural and sweet. Life becomes sweet.

• • •

When we call to Divine Mother in times of distress, we are rousing the presence of pure love within us, inviting the waters of compassion to douse the flames of sorrow. When we let go of clinging to sorrow, divine love finds its way in.

• • •

We can use our will to direct our thoughts in positive ways that are life and energy enhancing. Our persistent thoughts affect our emotions, over-all well-being, and energy levels. Use your thoughts to connect with the divine life and power within and around you. Affirm from that perspective that you are strong, vital, energetic, and enthusiastic. This will energize the body, lift your mood, and help you to be mentally clear. Thoughts seem insignificant but they are not. They are building blocks of power, subtle edifices of our present and future experience.

• • •

What use is a closed room full of jewels? When we reflect on it, our most treasured memories are occasions of giving in ways that enrich the joy of others. The things we hold onto pale in comparison.

• • •

With faith we understand that divine will is already accomplished. There is only the necessary work of showing up completely and removing whatever obstacles are there—a delightful job.

• • •

Set yourself free by setting others free.

• • •

Forgiveness has little to do with the person who has committed a wrong against us; it is about us and how we want to live. To forgive, or even to become willing to forgive, frees us. It brings us back into the present moment where peace is available and we are free to choose it.

• • •

Cultivating even-mindedness is like planting a garden—it takes time, patience, and dedication. If we allow ourselves to be overcome with anger, it is like pulling out the tender shoots by the root. Stand guard at the door of your mind. Do not allow negative thoughts to take root and grow.

• • •

When we are filled with divine love, we are unmoved by the passing opinions, actions, or words of others. What freedom we have in divine remembrance! Spiritual devotion takes the natural inclination of our hearts toward relationship and purifies it. This is how love becomes a way of freedom and not bondage, liberation and not attachment.

• • •

Divine grace is continually raining down in our lives. We put out a little bucket and when it doesn't catch much rain, we think something is wrong. Nothing is wrong. Get rid of the bucket. Step outside of limited thinking and stand in the downpour of divine grace and possibility.

• • •

Thoughts naturally arise. We cannot stop them. But we can change them. And changing our thoughts changes everything. When we change what we focus on, we change our experience of life. Freedom is not only freedom from something; it is freedom to bring in the new, the good that is waiting for the right conditions to arise.

• • •

Grace is inescapable blessing. It is always present but not always perceived. To uncover grace in our lives, we first assume that it is already at play through the many ways that we are supported by others, by circumstances, and by nature. Before long, a very real sense of being in the flow of grace arises.

• • •

The True Self is Unseen

The spiritual teacher knows who we are—beyond our personality, charm, cleverness, appearance, income, or intellectual prowess. The spiritual teacher not only sees the Divine within us, but also insists we realize it. The commitment of a true spiritual teacher is to call that forth and to settle for nothing less.

• • •

The spiritual teacher is the "cook," the one who helps us transform in the fire of tapas, or self-discipline. This transformation helps us actualize our potential and serve a higher purpose. We all have an inner pilot light, a tiny flame of awakened mind, awaiting the presence of an enlightened teacher to turn the flame up. Then the cooking of ego can begin.

• • •

When we let go of the illusion of owning an idea, a window opens and progress is ushered in, like a fresh and easy summer breeze.

• • •

When we are free of wanting or desiring, blessings easily appear and insights readily arise. Purity of heart prepares us for God-realization.

• • •

True prosperity rests upon realization of the spiritual principle of nonstealing, which brings freedom from envy, jealousy, and the desire for anything that does not rightfully belong to us. We do not envy, desire, or resent the good fortune of others because we realize our own sufficiency. When we know that we are capable of drawing all good that is for us, to us, we can truly celebrate the happiness and good fortune of others.

• • •

What we need may come to us in many different ways. It may come as insight, an awareness that allows us to know what to do. Or it may be something we read, or hear someone say. It could be a material gift that is given, or an opportunity that arises. The ways are truly infinite. Life continually supports the thriving, prospering, and fulfillment of its purposes. When we align our goals with serving the whole, we open the floodgates of grace-filled support.

• • •

Do what pleases the soul. Then self-discipline becomes a holy offering—sacrificing a lower drive for a higher one. Choose what is consistent with the truth of your being, and never settle for less.

• • •

Realizing the distinction between effort and intention is a formula for success.

• • •

Surrender of the sense of being separate from God frees us from the tyranny of self-will. Reliance on God is accomplished by continually turning the mind and heart toward divine remembrance. We let go of dependence on outer supports. We cannot depend on both.

• • •

Keep striving toward your goal with commitment, steadfast devotion to God, and even-mindedness in times of loss or gain. When all doors seem closed to you, know that God always leaves the door of healing open.

• • •

Like a mother who gives her child the toy he believes will bring him happiness, the spiritual teacher may assist devotees with their karma by helping them fulfill certain desires. Just as the mother knows the toy will soon be cast aside, so the teacher sees the student's steps before they are taken.

• • •

To look past hatred and see love, to look past separation and see unity, to look past loss and see gain—such are the ways of the spiritual warrior. Those who choose to live this way have dedicated themselves to realizing the light within themselves and calling it forth in the world.

• • •

Even in times of difficulty, the transformative work of the soul goes on. We are always connected to God whether we feel it to be so or not. The times when we are challenged to find our way are often the opening to a new chapter in our life inspired and supported by divine grace.

• • •

Inner Peace and Life Well Lived

Admitting we cannot do everything on our own
is the beginning of the soul's victory.

• • •

Wholeness is waiting to be discovered just beyond the
boundaries of our ego-based identity. No matter how
wonderful that outer identity is, without a conscious
connection to the Divine, it will always lack something. That something is the truth that sets us free.

• • •

Consider the possibility that you have the body that
is exactly right for your soul's journey in this lifetime,
the vehicle that will take you where you need to go,
providing the essential life experiences along the way
that support awakening to Self-realization. Love and
care for that body!

• • •

Refuge is always at hand. By letting go of the mistaken idea that we are separate from the One, we find shelter from any storm. The winds of worry and fear cannot enter the soul's fortress of peace.

• • •

Change your focus of attention, change your thinking, change your mind, and change your life. It only takes a moment. This moment is a good one.

• • •

It is possible to work hard, giving energy and attention to the task at hand, but without struggle. We struggle when we are trying to create something and imagine we are on our own. Train yourself to work first in consciousness before springing into action. The same body can fight strenuously, kicking feet, thrashing arms and hands to stay afloat in water—or relax and stay afloat effortlessly.

• • •

To live a magnificent life, cultivate a mind of wisdom, a heart of devotion, and hands of service.

• • •

Sadhana is like carrying a lamp into the dark night of our unconscious life. It reveals what is already there. It's easier to ignore the clutter of self-will and attachments that collect in our life if we do not bring the light to them. When we see what is there, we can make the changes that align with our higher Self.

• • •

There are so many different forms of meditation and various techniques. Which one is best? The one that pleases you. Choose a method or focus that resonates with you, stay with it. Trust yourself; follow your soul yearning.

• • •

In the *Bhagavad Gita,* the body is referred to as a city with nine gates—openings that are portals for sensory experience. In order for the city to be peaceful and beautiful there must be a city manager who knows the plan. This city manager is the purified ego—no longer in service to the personality, but in service to the soul, the governor.

• • •

At the core of our being, we are naturally peaceful. Notice if your thoughts become overly critical or judgmental, always looking for something that needs doing or fixing and never experiencing satisfaction. That is the mind influenced by the restless tendency in nature. Like a windstorm, it blows up a dust cloud of dissatisfaction. To calm this restless tendency in the midst of being active, use awareness of your breath to bring forth peace. A moment of mindful breathing will stop the storm.

• • •

When attention returns to abide in the Self, awareness moves from dwelling in the individual apartment of the body-mind to the omnipresent expanse of infinite joy, creative possibility, and pure knowledge. This is possible any time.

• • •

The spiritual plan for our lives is a living plan. It requires moment-to-moment participation. As we take the first step and follow guidance, the next step is revealed. Most of us would prefer to have the entire plan and its sure destination mapped out before we take that first step. But the spiritual way of life unfolds one surrendered step at a time.

• • •

To remain steadfast on the spiritual path requires commitment and a willingness to be teachable. We must be flexible, able to bend and even break open without giving up or losing heart. Think of willingness as complete openness to divine support. Open your heart and mind to the Infinite and ask for guidance. How often do we ask for guidance when we fall into a ditch of difficulty? Why not ask sooner rather than later?

• • •

Why should we cultivate dispassion when passion seems to connect us with feeling fully alive and involved with life? Dispassion supports our experience of aliveness while allowing us to be aware of the nuances of a situation that passion may obscure. Through practicing dispassion, we learn to remain nonreactive to changing conditions while we stay the course. Dispassion takes us off the roller coaster ride of the high of passion and its low ebb, which is often disappointment. Instead, it gives us the mental clarity and emotional availability that facilitates skillful action. This is essential for inner peace

• • •

Gratitude is not a feeling; it is an attitude. We can practice it regardless of how we feel in any given moment. When we cultivate a grateful attitude regardless of external conditions, we magnetize our awareness for good and contribute to peace. Gratitude turns us toward truth and frees us from self-preoccupation and worry.

• • •

People wonder: Is peace possible? When we experience our own transformation, we know it is possible. Let the soul's peace pervade the mind until thoughts become well-ordered and harmony prevails. How else will real peace come? Realize it—be it and bring it forth.

• • •

Restored to Our
Original Wholeness

One whose innate knowledge and exceptional abilities are fully awakened comprehends the wholeness of God and all souls as units of God's consciousness. Thus comprehending, one completely abandons the illusion of existence separate from God. This unification of awareness with God is the ultimate aim of every unenlightened soul.

—Sri Yukteswar

Everyday Enlightenment

As a lowly caterpillar knows to build a chrysalis of becoming, so are we guided toward awakening. The breaking of our shell is remembering what we are.

• • •

Through the practice of self-discipline and the influence of divine grace, it is possible for us to awaken and remember our true nature as spiritual beings. This is the purpose of life.

• • •

The path of wisdom:
Know everything.
Know nothing.
Know.

• • •

Spiritual awakening is an unfolding process, not a single event. As our consciousness changes, we change, and conditions in our lives change. This does not happen with one insight, but with heartfelt dedication and spirited determination to stay the course.

• • •

We are called to rise in great and small ways throughout our life. We never know the extent of our divine potential until a time or a situation arrives that both requires it of us and allows it to come forth. Everything—all of our experiences, our so-called successes and failures—brings us to such a moment of divine potential. When we witness grace in action, coursing through our life like a mighty river, any doubts we may have had about the greater Reality are dispelled. We are lifted up, carried to a new understanding, as we cooperate with the Infinite.

• • •

On the journey of spiritual awakening, nothing is ever wasted. The painful consequences of our errors can break our heart open and allow the true Self to shine the light of compassion into our life. Mistakes are like the bending branches of a beautiful tree—the way they keep turning toward the light. The seeming imperfection becomes its beauty.

• • •

Lovingkindness is not sentimental or a practice for the weak. It takes radical courage to meet life with an open heart, a clear mind, and a will to love.

• • •

The awakened life is not about becoming spiritual. It is not about gaining, or acquiring, becoming, or even regaining, something. We have never lost what we are. We may have forgotten; we may have lost touch with our true dignity and power, but we have never lost it. The Self does not wake up or go to sleep, come into being or pass from existence. It only seems so from the vantage point of "I," as the sun appears to the earth to rise and set, appear and disappear. Spiritual awakening changes the focal point of our lives from having to being. This is a radical reorientation, one that is essential to living a fulfilled life. Instead of thinking about what we want or need, we realize who we truly are.

• • •

Self-esteem is the natural blossoming of spiritual awakening. Immerse yourself in the awareness of the reality of God, and let that inner light contribute to right thinking about who you are. One who knows the truth is free from both the delusion of pride or of inferiority. It is not a matter of degrees. We either know who we are or we do not.

• • •

We express our divine nature by living it, by listening deeply to the soul's guidance and having the courage to follow it. The duty we are called to is precise and personal—the fulfillment of our own authentic self-expression. Even though we may carry out our role imperfectly, that is perfectly a part of the plan. Our imperfection is indispensable. It provides our growing edge.

• • •

Turn your thoughts to God with the intention of living in harmony with divine love, the law of your being. Then simply be present. Love will guide you. Love itself will introduce you to Supreme Love.

• • •

Spiritual progress does not come about purely through our own efforts, though they are necessary. Grace is essential for experiencing and living an awakened life. The winning combination of self-effort and divine grace assures our success. Do not expect God to get you out of bed in the morning, but expect Her to meet you in meditation.

• • •

It can be easy to get sidetracked and think our goal is about attaining or accomplishing something for its own sake. Viewed in the light of dharma, or higher purpose, our goals can be understood as the means for something much greater—a fully awakened life.

• • •

We thrive the moment we connect with the infinite Self. How could we not? We set ourselves on a steady course for this thriving to express outwardly by opening our mind to divine guidance, being receptive to our awakened intuition, and taking inspired action.

• • •

Spiritual practice requires continual course correction. Observing our thoughts and choices reveals the trend of our life. Are we aligning ourselves with peace or chasing after future fulfillment; living a life of zeal or succumbing to laziness or depression? Making useful changes when needed is how spiritual practice moves from the theoretical to the practical, from the sentimental to the real.

• • •

Healthy environments support us in remaining steadfast in our spiritual practice. It is necessary to set limits around indulging in addictions or moods—either our own or participating in those of others. Polish the body with cleansing practices. Polish the mind with patience. Polish the heart with contentment. Then your temple is ready for the divine Guest.

• • •

When we cannot discern between what brings sorrow and what brings lasting happiness, we have become confused by our desires and attachments. Buddhi—the discerning aspect of mind—is like an impartial judge who weighs input from the sensory cast of characters. Ego receives input from buddhi and decides which course of action is most beneficial to the self. A surrendered or purified ego and purified mind will choose the course of action that is in harmony with our soul.

• • •

Relating to others with compassion, engaging in work with integrity, and keeping our balance as we navigate life's changes—this is how we live spiritual teachings—moment to conscious moment.

• • •

Divine power within us is always ready to express through us to bring healing and expand our horizons beyond what we believe possible. We need only to trust and cooperate with it. Be unabashedly hopeful for your life and the life of our world. Let the language of your faith in God speak with every hopeful word and every constructive action.

• • •

Spiritual values are rising to the forefront of awareness for recognition and inclusion. How will we care for our children, for our earth? How will we integrate spiritual principles and nurture the soul in daily life? Parents who teach their children about the sacred nature of life help them to learn the true meaning of success. Those who lead the way will be the ones who follow the light of Spirit and let it shine through them into our world.

• • •

There is no greater healer than the Self.

• • •

To work for peace and nonviolence in our world is a useful focus for one who would practice karma yoga. Those attached to results either do not begin such work because they do not believe it is possible to achieve or they attempt to force solutions, ultimately contributing to the violence they would eradicate. Practicing karma yoga, or selfless service, one can begin.

• • •

Our first duty is to awaken to the truth of our being, then love and serve by beholding the One in all. The fulfillment of our nature requires it. It is the blossoming of our being. Just as an apple tree must bear apples to fulfill its potential, so divine love is our obligation of becoming. This awakening to love is a high demand. It requires us to forgive; it insists on putting others first; tells us we will be happier giving than receiving; says worry is a waste of time and we must trust life. This divine love is not emotion— it is an open-hearted awareness, the flowering of Self-knowledge.

• • •

Imagine your vital force, your energy, as a kind of currency you draw upon and put to use. Consider ways to conserve this energy, use it wisely, and avoid wasting it. Purposeful living is the starting place for enhancing vital force. Without a clear focus in life, we are apt to wander aimlessly through our days and spill away our energy. This is akin to spending money wherever we go without any thought or consideration of our income or bank balance. A sure path to bankruptcy. Being ever mindful of our goal of spiritual realization keeps us from getting distracted and wasting time and energy. A sure path to wealth beyond measure.

• • •

You are divine. Wake up from the mortal dream and live as an enlightened being. Why put it off by imagining it is not possible for you? Enlightenment is the revelation of our essential nature, unimpeded by false identification. Enlightenment already is.

• • •

The Power of Truthful Living

Humility is right relationship with life. It is recognizing ourselves and others as individualized expressions of one infinite Reality. Every flower, every snowflake, every star, every person, is uniquely the same. Each expression of Spirit is awesomely unique and yet the same essence is within all. Why compare yourself to anyone else?

• • •

The invitation to realize oneness, to experience divine love and support, is always present but sometimes we miss it. We get distracted, or worried, or too self-concerned to consider that there is something magnificent going on. There is. We all have hints that there is more to us, more to life. Something greater, vaster, richer, and deeper. This persistent inclination to look for "something more" is the soul seeking to realize itself. Be like a miner following a vein of gold; follow that inclination to its source.

• • •

Love is the mighty ocean of God's presence.
Forgiveness is the river that finds its way
to that ocean.

• • •

Consider the power of truthful living expressed through simple, profound acts. What is one thing you can do that supports healing, reveals harmony and the presence of peace? Do that. Do not put it off. Draw on the wellspring of infinite creativity.

• • •

Every day we build the temple of our lives—thought by thought, word by word, deed by deed. Let your mind be a temple for worshipping God, your thoughts candles of praise.

• • •

We can enjoy life as we cooperate with our unfolding potential and highest good. We do not have to put off joy, thinking of it as a result of any accomplishment or acquisition. Unconditional joy, or bliss, is a quality of the soul. When we are in touch with that, we are in touch with the soul.

• • •

We cannot control the thoughts that enter the stream of the mind. However, we do have a choice about what we will dwell on, what we will believe, what we will act on, and what we will allow to remain. Spiritual mastery begins with these choices.

• • •

Dana, or charitable giving, is an opportunity to change our consciousness from scarcity to plenty— from being separate and apart to being directly connected to the source of all good. Dana is very similar to establishing a meditation practice. We commit ourselves to giving on a regular basis to support a worthy cause because of who we are and our relationship to life. We do not give because we feel like giving. We give because we know we are not separate from the source of all giving. Through giving, we slip into the stream and become part of its mighty flow.

• • •

Begin to live now as the person you desire to be. Since experiences unfold from beliefs, states of mind, and consciousness, start there. If your intention is to experience a loving relationship, then imagine, see, and know yourself as a loving person. Speak and act as a loving person would.

• • •

Success is the child of commitment.

• • •

We are all destined for the ultimate success of liberation of consciousness—the absolute freedom that unfolds from Self-realization. Along the way, let us encourage one another and surround ourselves with those who bring out the best in us. To measure success, ask: *Did I remember God? How well did I love? Did I support others along the way? Was I kind and generous?*

• • •

There are no short cuts to prosperity. We cannot fully prosper by going against our deepest values. As we consider how to thrive, let it be in ways that are supportive of the soul. A simple way to prosper is to do what we know is the best thing to do each day; do it with the devotion for God that makes the heart sing and the soul rejoice.

• • •

To heal from the erroneous belief of insufficiency— not having or being enough—remember your true nature. Right where you are, whatever your situation, the resources necessary to transform your life are at hand. Turn doubts into devotion by surrendering into the sufficiency of God in, and as, your life.

• • •

To discover your life purpose, simply pay attention. Pay attention to your basic nature, your gifts, talents, and responsibilities. What makes your heart sing with joy? What brings you peace? As an apple seed becomes an apple tree and not a pine tree, our life purpose is to develop our unique potential by expressing who we are authentically. Every person is spiritually designed and destined for success. Turn toward the truth of your being and boldly embrace your divine identity. Cultivate fearlessness by trusting your Self completely.

• • •

Practicing patience is like coming upon a cool stream on a hot day—the overheated ego stops, cools down, and reconnects with the soul nature.

• • •

Prayer for the workplace: *God be my day planner today. Help me to remember that You are present in every meeting and that all work is for Your sake. When I see my co-workers I will think only of You. I will put them first as I offer my service to You. The workplace will be my practice hall today.*

• • •

No matter how much we have, we will only have enough when we have enough to give. It is not possible to ever accumulate enough to be full if we do not give. It seems illogical, yet it is true that our sufficiency rests on our generosity.

• • •

Three things are needed for success on the spiritual path: commitment to the goal of realization, receptivity to instruction and to grace, and dedicated practice.

• • •

It is futile to fight our divine nature. Once we become aware of the battle between the drive of the ego for self-preservation and the inspiring uprising of the soul nature toward truth, surrender is the only real option. It is the choice for enduring happiness.

• • •

We can see where we are headed if we observe where we are right now. What is experienced now is due to past causes. Like a well-tended field, a life of happiness grows from the careful work of cultivating contentment. Kind thoughts and compassionate actions bring peace to us in the moment and plant the seeds of future happiness.

• • •

Patience is a friend of true possibility. When we are patient, we wait for the time and the means of right action to appear.

• • •

The antidote for regret is to bring awareness into the present moment. Consider what you can do now that makes a difference and do it. A sure way to free yourself from the past is to step out of it with right action.

• • •

When the light of inner wisdom dawns and we are able to act with heart, mind, and soul in alignment, then it is time to move forward. Until then, receptive stillness is the way.

• • •

Choose words carefully. Speech is a creative power. We affirm and call forth conditions and experiences with the words we speak and the beliefs that support them. Speech is a bridge between the subtle realm of thought and the material realm of things. They are not separate, they are a continuum, intricately connected—thoughts, words, things, circumstances.

• • •

Just like a verdant garden, the spiritual life requires tending. We may want the "quick fix" but nothing replaces daily, patient, practice as the quickest and most efficient way of hastening a life in tune with God's divine plan. We weed out self-limiting beliefs and non-useful behaviors, set good boundaries around people or circumstances that deplete our energy or distract us from our primary purpose, and make sure we include the life-giving waters of spiritual study and daily exposure to the light of the soul in superconscious meditation. These are all necessary practices to harvest a healthy, harmonious, happy life.

• • •

Sitting on our meditation seat, studying scripture, charitable giving, and selflessly serving others are all part of spiritual living. The crux of it takes place in the moment-to-moment choices we make each day. Look for those opportune times when a moment of prayer, or mindfulness, will bring more spiritual awareness to your day—times such as entering and leaving your home, beginning work, answering the phone, or eating a meal. It takes only a moment to invite the light.

• • •

Turn the mind. Curb the tongue. Open the heart.

• • •

If you catch yourself thinking that you need someone else's approval, or wanting something with the idea that you'll be improved, come back to awareness of your divine Self. Say to yourself: *I am full. I am whole. I am complete.* Remember.

• • •

Every cell of our body is vibrant with divine power and wisdom. Learn to listen to its music; attend to its prompts toward right action. Though the body continually sends out signals and clues for self-care and balanced living, too often we ignore those signals. We neglect to eat when we are hungry or sleep when we are tired. Learning to discern and heed the simple promptings of body wisdom is profoundly more important than accumulating information about healthy living. Study the book of your daily life, the signals of the body, the nudges of your conscience. Witness the way your heart opens into the beauty of the day, given enough space.

• • •

Create order and spaciousness in your environment and you will naturally feel more calm and open. Our physical space is an extension of our body and mind. Choose carefully what you let in the door of your home or office. Tending to our physical space is not separate from our spiritual practice. A mindful practice, a mindful space.

• • •

It is up to us to make choices that are consistent with being awake. We can decide whether to fulfill our soul's destiny or allow ourselves to be swept away by the tide of our circumstances. Intentional living focused on spiritual awakening keeps us living the divine life.

• • •

We are lifted out of the past—out of fear, worry, or lack, and out of bondage to any condition—when we cease identifying ourselves with the condition.

• • •

We can push a shopping cart forward even if a wheel is out of alignment, but it takes more energy to do it. When we are conflicted, our energy is dissipated by doubt. Set a clear intention to follow truth as a way to align your thoughts, speech, and action then glide with grace. Enjoy action as your offering. Do it as delight, as play in the field of the Lord.

• • •

There is no doubt that the spiritual path is arduous. It is like swimming upstream against a strong current. Many times we are dashed against the rocks of doubt and self-will. Yet those who persevere find serene pools of peace, restful to the soul. Ultimately the vast reservoir of truth is found. Let your mind be glad and your heart enraptured by turning toward the One.

• • •

Strive for Self-realization rather than self-improvement. Simply inquiring, *Am I sincere?* before acting is powerful. We know the answer, if we only stop and ask. Sincerity makes the joy of conscious living possible.

• • •

Notice the emphasis placed on listening in the spiritual traditions—Krishna tells Arjuna, "Listen to my Supreme Word." Jesus says, "My sheep will hear my voice." The sacred Jewish prayer begins, "Hear O Israel." What is it to listen, to hear and become receptive, a vessel, an opening? Surrender to the wisdom of listening.

• • •

If you find yourself procrastinating, holding back, delaying, or not wanting to do what you know you should do, use it as an opportunity to strengthen your commitment to your purpose and discover what is holding you back. Instead of giving in to this tendency, hold it up to the light of awareness, then take a step. One step is all it takes to break procrastination's spell.

• • •

Using our discernment before we acquire something by deciding if it is truly beneficial is not only wise, it keeps our soul life in the forefront of our awareness. Every desire is energy in motion. To discern whether a desire is useful or not, follow its trajectory. Where does it lead? What is the likely outcome?

• • •

Abide in the Self

Both wisdom and devotion are spiritual paths to the summit of ultimate Truth. Although these paths have a different emphasis and approach, that is only different scenery along the way. They have the same goal. Once the summit of clear seeing is attained, the paths converge. Ultimate knowledge leads to devotion while true devotion brings wisdom.

• • •

We may fail to notice our own contentment if we get too busy chasing after things. True contentment does not arise in response to any circumstance. It arises when the mind is calm and the joy of the soul is revealed. Knowing this, we are reminded to seek happiness where we are most likely to find it—in the temple of superconscious meditation.

• • •

Discernment beyond initial impressions is necessary to determine whether our thoughts and actions will lead to happiness or sorrow. Lust and greed may be pleasurable in the beginning but end in pain. Compassion and kindness are sometimes painful in the beginning but end in happiness.

• • •

Emotion experienced without wisdom and detachment swells like an overflowing stream in a rain storm. Accept that emotion brings wisdom. With discernment, its wisdom can be accessed like drawing water from a well. Just avoid falling in.

• • •

We are often advised that in order to succeed and have our needs met, we should work harder or work smarter by better time management or improving our skills. Both can be useful, yet the highest way to prosper is to focus our attention on our relationship with Spirit. When we do that, all else follows and our needs are easily provided for. Work done with devotion to God has success naturally built into it.

• • •

The approach to meditation requires some initial expenditure of energy like an airplane on the runway that builds speed and energy to the point of lift off. Concentration on a single point of focus is the approach to meditation. It prepares the way. Meditation begins when the effort required to concentrate gives way to a steady flow of attention and the mental field has become calm. Meditation is above the clouds of thought.

• • •

Establishing a routine of meditation is similar to beginning an exercise program. At first the body and mind resist; then the positive benefits begin to influence our decision-making process. When the subtle pleasure, or bliss, of meditation permeates the mental field we begin to want to meditate and we miss it if we stop. Others we live with also notice the positive changes in our demeanor and interactions. They become inclined to remind us to return to our practice if we lose our balance.

••••

Most people imagine their career as their real work and spiritual practice as an adjunct. For those dedicated to Self- and God-realization, the imaginary line of separation between spiritual practice and work is erased. When work is understood as service, the questions of right livelihood are more easily answered. Service contributes to the welfare of others, to peace, and to the repair and healing of the world. Any vocation that is contrary to these cannot be called right livelihood. See your spiritual practice as your real work and it will rightly guide what you do.

••••

Amassing "spiritual" knowledge without knowledge of oneself is useless. We are simply parrots who have learned words. True spiritual knowledge dispels ignorance of our essential nature. Once that error is corrected, our study becomes fruitful.

• • •

Our word is imbued with divine power. It goes forth precisely as we have sent it to blossom and bear fruit according to its nature. Its nature is of the thought, the belief, and the intention behind it. When we choose our words carefully and follow through with what we say, we build confidence in the power of our word. We discover the spiritual power of truth.

• • •

We can dedicate our home as a place of blessing. With the intention to bless, we welcome every guest as God. We are then more likely to act in accordance with our divine nature—to be generous, patient, and kind.

• • •

Pay close attention to the mistakes you make and overlook those of others. While it is possible to learn from the mistakes of others, our own errors contain the most potential for transforming our character.

• • •

We perform many supportive acts for ourselves every day without expecting any acknowledgement. With spiritual vision, we can care for others in the same way—spontaneously and without expecting a return.

• • •

Five practices for spiritually healthy relationships: Keep your attention on God. Let go of the need to be right. Practice positive speaking that uplifts. Cultivate even-mindedness. Be kind.

• • •

Avoid falling into the spiritual trap of working on yourself to become spiritual. Only ego tries to get rid of ego. When the fallibility of ego is seen, an opening occurs for supportive grace to pour in. Be awake: live in peace; live in joy.

• • •

In a heart made whole by surrender, the dark night of grief heralds the dawn of new life. Be willing to sit in the silence and wait upon the direct perception of the higher Self. Once released from identification with the body, mind, and emotions, soar in the freedom of Spirit and experience new vistas of possibility opening before you.

• • •

Who is our friend? Who is our enemy? The same person can play both roles. Who hasn't had a lover or a friend betray their trust? When this happens, the admirable qualities of that person seem to vanish overnight. Was this person the reason for our joy? Are they now the reason for our sorrow? Realize the true source of joy and be free. There is a joy we can know and retain no matter what occurs. This joy is innate to the soul. We have it always. The secret is to refuse to let anyone or anything take it away.

• • •

The self-serving motives of ego are destroyed by serving others; releasing strong desires for specific results; not reacting to praise or blame; and giving with no thought of receiving in return.

• • •

True knowledge and humility are inseparable companions. They do everything together.

• • •

Good works are useful to a point, but they can also be an obstacle to our awakening. If there is attachment to our work—the desire to gain praise, favor with God, or an enlightened state through what we do, then it becomes a detriment. For an action to be pure it must be accomplished purely throughout. When all that we do, all our encounters (with everyone and everything) is for the sake of God-realization, the attachment to particular outcomes falls away. When the only outcome desired is awakening, whatever happens can serve that purpose.

• • •

Instead of asking for things to be different when facing difficulty, pray to know what is true. Ask to see clearly the way things are and be willing to change. Then it becomes possible to cooperate with the highest good.

• • •

God meets our needs through us with our conscious participation. Needs are not met by asking God for things as if God were a parent dispensing goods to a child. Our needs are met by seeking the wisdom and insight to discern clearly the divine idea that holds the plan for us. The divine idea will show the way to meet the need.

• • •

There are many things in life that we cannot change or control but we do have the power to transform our minds and thus, our experience of life. We can become more patient, kind, insightful, and compassionate. Let us encourage one another with spiritual friendship, conversations that are uplifting, and remembrance of our true purpose in life.

• • •

The spiritual teacher ferries the boat that takes us across the river of delusion. Attachment to the teacher is natural in the beginning, but once the shore of divine realization is reached, we relinquish that attachment so that inner wisdom may guide us.

• • •

The desire to know and serve God supports the unfolding of our innate potential. Service is a vehicle for awakening only if approached selflessly. Watch for signs of seeking appreciation or acknowledgement and release those impediments. Selfless service can be identified by pure intent, a motive that is free from selfishness; the ability to remain even-minded in times of loss or gain, praise or blame; and depth of caring for the means of the work while surrendering the result. The joy of doing work for God is its own astounding reward.

• • •

When spiritual wisdom ripens, past deeds drop away like flower petals before fruit. True wisdom changes us. We no longer live as we did in the past. A new life begins.

• • •

The Awakened Life

The soul is already blissful. Our urge to find and experience lasting happiness is our yearning to actualize our innate joy—to know it, live it, realize it. When we realize that what we are looking for is actually within us, we can focus on how to express what we are, rather than trying to find something that we have never lost.

• • •

Begin the day knowing that whatever you need is already on its way to you. Be mindful of the divine inspiration that awaits your cooperation to be expressed. Be ready and willing. Greet people and events as divine messengers and enjoy the play of life.

• • •

What is your dream? What would you do if you were not afraid to do it? If you believed that you were connected to the source of infinite possibility and supply? If you recognized Spirit as both the source of the dream and the means to achieve it?

• • •

To live prosperously is to vow to grow. The focus is not on having more, burdening the self with more responsibility and attachments, but on being more— more aware, more alive, more joyous, and free. This is prosperity—to know and realize that we are innately prosperous, that thriving is the natural expression of our divinity. God's omnipotence, divine creative energy and power, indwells everyone. It is full; it lacks nothing. Like you.

• • •

What power is contained in our imagination! Through creative use of our imagination, divine inspiration moves into physical manifestation. Use imagination to bring forth prosperity, peace, and joy. It will bridge the inner and outer expression of Spirit.

• • •

The mind purified by prayer, meditation, and surren- dered devotion becomes like a transparent jewel. It shines with the light of the soul and reflects divine inspiration.

• • •

Those who are wise change their lives by changing their consciousness—changing themselves from the inside out.

• • •

The purpose of the outer teacher or guru is to lead us home to the true Guru, the divine Self. An enlightened teacher can transmit spiritual truth to the receptive student because that same truth already resides within her. The eternal truth is within us all. The teacher's grace helps the seeker to discover God's grace. Ultimately, however, our own grace is required for liberation. Those who are willing to thrive, to live their lives to their fullest potential, invite into their life the activity of grace in its three aspects—as God, as the teacher, and as the true Self.

• • •

Prayer is the best way to begin and end the day, but even better—the best way to live throughout the day. Again and again, redirect your attention from thoughts—from considerations of this or that—into your heart, your essence of being.

• • •

Our energy, vigor, and inner strength increase as we progress on the spiritual path. When we exercise our dynamic wisdom-guided will, break old habits and patterns, take new positive actions, and move through obstacles, our fortitude grows. Nothing brings such strength as the will to awaken.

• • •

The ability to concentrate—to focus our attention, awareness, and energy on one thing at a time—unlocks our soul power, which is the power to manifest our worthy goals. When we immerse ourselves in the unbounded essential Self in superconscious meditation, that expansiveness continues to pervade our consciousness throughout the day. It helps us stay open to insight, remain centered, and be guided by divine grace. This is the inner way of arranging conditions for success.

• • •

The joyous, spiritually-conscious life rests upon simple choices—choices made in ordinary moments each day. Choosing well is living well.

• • •

Our particular work already exists in the divine plan. When we bring forth our innate potential to match it, we cannot miss it. Attend to the inspirations that arise within you. Pay attention to your intuition. Notice.

• • •

When we do not need to possess the beauty we encounter, we can experience it with radical amazement.

• • •

Give up the search for lasting happiness
and claim it instead.

• • •

Contemplate the possibility of enlightenment now. Try it on and get used to it. Contemplating enlightenment is not the same as experiencing it, but it can be a helpful way to open ourselves to our potential. Cease thinking enlightenment is only for a select few. The same Self, the same infinite potential, is within all.

• • •

Even one experience of samadhi, or supercon-sciousnes, nurtures us many times—first by being immersed in the bliss of the divine Self, then as memory. During times of seeming separation, the sweet recollection of inner communion returns to sustain us, lifting us once again to higher awareness.

• • •

Do not let the opportunity for a blessing pass you by. Practice flexing your inspiration muscles by acting on your insights. When you discern that your intu-ition is in harmony with the highest good for all concerned, why hesitate?

• • •

No one, not even the saints, reaches enlightenment through action. But action is necessary. Do not imagine yourself as the doer—this is the passport to skillful action. Rest in the awareness of God as the owner of all outcomes. Engage in action that is clear and deliberate from the start to the finish—free from the murky restlessness that comes from attachment to particular results.

• • •

Live your life as a great bliss adventure. Be willing to follow what has heart and meaning. Let go of any attachment to how you think it should be and allow the soul to lead. Trust your intuition by following it.

• • •

Nothing occurs that cannot bring us closer to God-realization. Everything that happens is an invitation to discover the truth. Whether engaged in action in the world, or the stillness of meditation, it can be our goal to know the truth and live it. There are no mundane days for those whose hearts are on fire to realize God.

• • •

Prayer makes responding to a situation possible where only reacting existed before. When our first step is prayer, the next step will be divinely directed.

• • •

When the surrendered heart is broken open, the underground stream of divine love rises to the surface and washes everything clean. Life shines anew.

• • •

By accepting our responsibility as agents of our own life experience we empower ourselves to make positive changes. Real change happens through a change of consciousness. Insight is then reflected in our thoughts, words, and actions. A true change of heart is revealed by new attitudes and behavior. We hold the formula of our own empowerment.

• • •

When the call to awaken comes, we may feel it as sweetness, or even as grief—it comes in many forms. In whatever way we experience it, it is an indication that the divine teacher is near.

• • •

Prayer begins in the mind, moves to the heart, and finally to the feet.

• • •

Prayer of the heart is a prayer that arises spontaneously from divine love. When we are in love, there is no effort required to think of our beloved—our mind is captured by the heart.

• • •

A devotee on the enlightenment path doesn't try to control, change, or convert others, but instead looks to see what adjustment is necessary in his or her own mind and consciousness to bring about harmony. The influence of a single transformed life is beyond calculation; it ripples out and touches the lives of countless others. An entire family can be healed or transformed by one person who is spiritually awake.

• • •

On the spiritual path we live by the great agenda, which is to awaken to Truth and discern God's will. Our personal agenda—our goals, plans, and dreams—is second to this. Spiritual maturity is marked by recognition and observance of this greater way to live.

• • •

Love and ethics work together. Like our two legs, both are needed for balance and for our ability to walk through the world. Without ethics, love can be blind and without love, ethics can be a set of outer-directed rules. Together they are powerful. Accompanied by spiritual awakening, they are unbeatable.

• • •

Neither austerity nor luxury brings lasting happiness. The wealth of an awakened heart full of divine love is the only currency that provides enduring joy.

• • •

The Supreme Teacher is Divine Consciousness residing within us. The outer teacher is the mirror that shows us this truth. Some hesitate at the doorway of the guru-disciple relationship, afraid that the mirror will reflect their flaws. But those who go through that door with courage, discover that the guru reveals the luminous Self that was hidden for so long.

• • •

Awaken each day to the song of divine remembrance ever singing in the soul. Greet the dawn with the colors of your own magnificence. Step out into the day with the vitality that flows from the radiant source of your being. Do not hold back. Let it shine.

• • •

About the Author

Yogacharya Rev. Ellen Grace O'Brian, M.A., is a teacher, writer, and spiritual director of the Center for Spiritual Enlightenment (CSE) with headquarters in San Jose, California, USA. CSE is a Kriya Yoga Meditation Center serving people from all faith backgrounds who are seeking Self- and God-realization. She was ordained to teach in 1982 by Roy Eugene Davis, a direct disciple of Paramahansa Yogananda who brought Kriya Yoga from India to the West.

Yogacharya O'Brian has taught yoga philosophy and meditation practices for spiritually-conscious living at retreats, spiritual centers, and conferences throughout the US and internationally for over three decades. She is the author of several books on spiritual practice, including *Living the Eternal Way: Spiritual Meaning and Practice in Daily Life,* as well as three volumes of poetry including the forthcoming title from Homebound Publications, *The Moon Reminded Me.* She writes regularly for *Truth Journal* magazine, is the editor of *Enlightenment Journal,* a quarterly yoga magazine, and host of *The Yoga Hour,* a weekly radio program and podcast with Unity Online Radio.

She is the Founder and President of *Meru Institute,* offering certification programs, leadership training, and education in Yoga, Ayurveda, and Community Ministry since 1996 and Carry the Vision, a community education nonprofit organization teaching principles and practices of ahimsa (nonviolence) to all sectors of society. Yogacharya O'Brian served as the Vice Chair of the Board of Trustees of the Parliament of the World's Religions and is a recipient of several community service awards, including the prestigious 2015 Mahatma Gandhi Award for the Advancement of Religious Pluralism by the Hindu American Foundation. She lives in Santa Cruz, California with her husband, Michael. They have three fabulous grown children and two precocious grandchildren.

About CSE

The **Center for Spiritual Enlightenment,** founded in 1981, is a meditation center in the spiritual tradition of Kriya Yoga. The Center ministry welcomes people from all backgrounds who are seeking Self- and God-realization—a path to spiritually-conscious, fulfilled living in the world. The teachings offered at CSE have their origins in the ancient Vedas, which offer a universally applicable path for spiritual awakening relevant to our time. To realize the truth of our essential nature and live in the highest way is the goal of the path. Every day, both locally and globally, for over thirty-five years, the CSE ministry has continued to offer spiritual teachings and practical support to all who are seeking a spiritually awakened life.

CSE World Headquarters is located in San Jose, California, where meditation instruction, Kriya Yoga teachings and initiation, worship services, hatha yoga classes, youth spiritual education, ministry services, and retreats are regularly offered. It is also the home of *Meru Institute,* founded in 1996 to train teachers and leaders in the Kriya Yoga tradition by offering educational programs in yoga studies, Ayurveda, and community ministry; a meditation garden that is open daily to the public; CSE Press; Lahiri House for private and small group meditation retreats; and a welcome center and bookshop.

CSE shares inspiration and teachings globally by offering weekly online radio programs, online classes (live streaming and archived), daily email inspirations, publications, and outreach teaching.

www.CSEcenter.org

info@csecenter.org

1146 University Avenue
San Jose, California 95126

CSE Press

CSE Press was established in 1998 to provide an avenue for publication of the Kriya Yoga teachings offered by Yogacharya O'Brian. The first book published, *Living the Eternal Way: Spiritual Meaning and Practice for Daily Life* is still being offered nearly two decades later. It remains the primary text for the *Living the Eternal Way* course, an introduction to the philosophy and practices of Kriya Yoga.

A Single Blade of Grass: Finding the Sacred in Everyday Life, a selection of inspirational sayings and introduction to the core practices, was published in 2002 and remains in circulation as well.

CSE Press has diversified over the years to include publication of an illustrated book for all ages titled *Once Before Time,* a creation story, as well as several CD collections of inspirational messages on the spiritual classics such as the *Bhagavad Gita, the Gospel of Thomas,* and the *Upanishads.*

Largely run by volunteers, CSE Press distributes books and other materials both nationally and internationally.

To subscribe to Daily Inspirations,
visit: www.CSEcenter.org or
write: info@csecenter.org